The Impossibility ZONE

Where Faith Triumphs!

Dannie Hood

Evergreen
PRESS

ISBN 1-58169-188-2
For Worldwide Distribution
Printed in the U.S.A.

Evergreen Press
P.O. Box 191540 • Mobile, AL 36619
800-367-8203

Table of Contents

DEDICATION

I want to dedicate this book to my mother.
She taught me at a young age that
love is the true energy of endurance.

ACKNOWLEDGMENTS

Thanks to my wife
for the comfort of undying love

To my kids
for engendering countless smiles

To my numerous friends
for supporting my dreams

To my mentors, Billy Hale and Thomas Craft
for being anchors of integrity

To Brian and Kathy Banashak
for timely advice and insightful editing

To Keith Carroll for helping me
get through another door

Most of all, to my Savior Jesus
for giving me more than I ever deserved

Foreword

The Impossibility Zone is a book with cultural relevance for the 21st Century. It goes to the very heart of the dreamer who is not satisfied with the status quo, who wants to think and live outside the box of religious limitations.

The world is waiting for people who have traveled through the Impossibility Zone to bring a message of hope to the world community, to pursue the dreams and passions placed in them by God.

Dannie Hood adequately depicts the faith-formula for the Impossibility Zone: moving forward despite conflict, following your dream no matter the struggle, and fulfilling a vital role as a witness to the provisional grace of God.

In this book you discover the key to becoming a blessing to God, others, and yourself. You will be a blessing to God because you will represent Him the way He wants to be seen. You will be a blessing to others because you will help them see the route to true joy. And you will be a blessing to yourself because you will live truly fulfilled in your relationship with God.

— Andrew Tennyson
Liaison Officer for Compassion Services Int'l

Chapter One

On the Path of Impossibility

Have you ever thought or said these words: "It's impossible! I'll never find an escape from my circumstances. I don't know how I will ever find a way to be happy or at peace"?

If so, you may be in the impossibility zone of past mistakes, present pain, or future fear. In II Kings 6 and 7 there is a story filled with horror and hope, of impossibility and miracles. I believe that you will find a thread of hope in it, and when you see that thread, pull it; you just may begin to unravel the pattern of impossibility that hell is trying to weave around you.

Samaria, during the time of II Kings 6, was a land of olive vineyards, barley and wheat fields. The hills of Samaria were lush with produce — some of the best farming land in all of Israel. Not far from the illustrious gates of the city was the valley of barley, a fertile bowl of abundant producing land. In the middle of the valley rose a hill, several miles wide — a rocky finger pointing toward the city's enemies in the north. To the west of Samaria, watchmen stood atop towers of defense,

1

looking down on the yellow thread of coastal shoreline, and the tumbling white-capped waves of the Great Sea.

From the north came the tyrannical Ben-hadad and his army. Ben-hadad fiercely ruled Syria, and his thirst for blood was insatiable. His army encamped against fear-stricken Samaria. The intimidating soldiers dressed in war regalia, blinding the men on the watchtowers with the reflection off their silver, cone-shaped helmets. The Syrian soldiers grasped their swords firmly, eager to spill the blood of Jews.

No one could leave the city to get food. The Syrians had barricaded every exit, with soldiers standing ready to kill anyone who tried. Conditions inside the city walls were horrific. Starvation quickly set in. A donkey's head was bartered for 80 pieces of silver, the modern day equivalent of 50 dollars. Even babies were cooked and served as a cannibalistic dish of survival. Having cut them off from all food sources, the Syrians believed the Jews' surrender to be imminent. The economy was in chaos, the morale of the city degraded, and the government was relegated to blaming a man of God named Elisha.

While the citizens of Samaria were starving, a plan was developing outside the gates of the city. Four lepers, dressed in soiled, threadbare garments, sat calculating their chances of survival. These men were the outcasts of society, a group of diseased victims who had no hope of ever enjoying the privileges of citizenship again.

Each day, their skin ulcers worsened, the numbness in their limbs increased, and even their collective will to live deteriorated at the sight of the horrifying reflection of themselves, whether in a pool of water or a brazen dish.

I imagine they dreaded the sunrise some mornings, wondering what part of their anatomy might have been affected by the disease during the night. No doubt they feared the spreading of gangrene to yet another finger, or, even worse, developing a state of total paralysis that would leave them helpless, doomed to rotting in the sun — not yet dead, but still undesirable.

However, even in the midst of all this, there was one positive thing in their lives: they had each other. They were citizens on the same island of despair and subscribers to the same documents of earthly rejection. They lived with each other's stench. They no doubt drank from a communal cup and occasionally mustered up enough good humor to laugh about catching some minor sickness like a cold.

At some point during their discussions, an aroma of rotisserie lamb wafted through the air, pervading their senses, reawakening their taste buds, and filling their hearts with a bit of hope.

"That sure smells better than Lefty's armpit," joked one of the lepers. (Lefty was, of course, the leper who had lost his right arm to the disease.)

They knew the appetizing smell came from the festive camp of the Syrians. And while their stomachs growled and images of sumptuous meals filled their heads, they looked at one another as if an angelic formula for survival had just been laid in their laps.

One of the lepers finally spoke up, with a new resolve.

Why should we wait here until we die? It's no use going into the city, because we would starve to death in there; but if we stay here, we'll die also. So let's go to the Syrian camp; the worst they can do is kill us, but maybe they will spare our lives (II Kings 7:4 TEV).

It's interesting that he said, "The worst they can do is. . ." Isn't that phrase a sign of true desperation? In my own life, when things seem truly futile, I find myself repeating that very phrase: "The worst they can do is. . . say no. . .take my last dollar. . .leave. . .fire me. . .say that the alternative medicine won't work." At the same time, strangely, the worst-case scenario offers a glimmer of hope. True, it's a confession that reveals being at our wit's end — the sense that one has lost an opportunity. It is the place where the hands are thrown up, but it also can be the place where the gauntlet is thrown down, and caution is thrown to the wind. It is often the final agreement with God and one's circumstances that the only way to go is forward — no matter what the outcome. So the first lesson the lepers teach us is that the only thing to do on the path of impossibility is to *go forward.*

Rather than rot in a state of predetermined misery, the lepers resolved to *take a risk* on finding mercy. In the same way, there may be some people who will declare that you are unfit and not salvageable, thus writing you off as spiritually dead. But the Word of the Lord says, "His mercy endures forever." God's compassion is never-ending. If you feel trapped at the gates with no one else to count on, do what the lepers did: *take a chance on mercy.* Just as the one leper realized that going back to the city was useless, dwelling on our past failures is equally useless, and only leads to condemnation. Take a chance on God's mercy. Move forward. You never know what bounty of grace may wait ahead.

With nothing but the aftertaste of dust and stale bread in their mouths, the lepers set out on this nothing-to-lose journey and entered the impossibility zone. Cottony clouds moved in unison along their predetermined path. The patches of clear sky appeared even bluer to the leprous travelers. The coarse dirt felt no different beneath their shuffling feet, except for the anticipation of what lay ahead.

The lepers had to cover about one-half mile before they would become visible to the Syrian camp. Methodically they moved up the steady incline, hearts pounding faster, like the rising beat of war drums. They were leaving behind the empty cupboards of constancy and heading toward abundance in the realm of danger. Behind them lay a slow death and certain graves. Before them lay the chance to encounter mercy and swallow savory meat with a goblet full of fresh juice from the vine. Would they be considered unwelcome trespassers and hanged, or humble traders, accepted and able to barter their misery for a taste of mercy?

Meanwhile, in the Syrian camp, a sudden disturbance interrupted the soldiers' meal. Alarmed, a guard stood to his feet and cocked his head toward the hills. What he heard sent a deathly chill down his spine. Others stopped talking and also began to listen. On an angelic wind of delusion came the sound of countless chariots. The thunderous hooves, the jostling sounds of iron chariots driven hard, the crumbling of rocks, and the gruff shouts of captains were all part of the divine special effects the Almighty had orchestrated.

The sound of approaching warriors set off a Syrian stampede of panic. Leaving their legs of lamb half-eaten and flasks of wine leaking blood-red in the sand, the hurrying Syrians fled with only their clothes on their back. Gold, silver, and fine silk garments were ignored in their haste to save their lives.

The Syrians believed that Hittite and Egyptian warriors, hired by the king of Israel, were their unseen attackers, so they fled the scene before they could be ambushed. In only a matter of minutes, the Syrian camp became a ghost town. Not one Syrian was left, only the horses and donkeys, some flapping tent canvasses, a few crackling logs on the fire, and a squawking buzzard perched on a nearby stump.

A few moments later, the four lepers topped the hill above the Syrian camp. Bewilderment played across each leper's face as he scanned the surroundings. The men had stepped into the realm of the miraculous. They were not yet aware that God had orchestrated a coup against the Syrians. God's secret became their celebration.

They quickly entered the camp and proceeded to eat like kings. The men devoured their food like ravenous beasts in the forest. They sniffled and slurped; they chewed briskly and belched often. They laughed and cried, tears mixing with smudge marks of roasted meat on their cheeks.

God took their step of faith and gave them a feast. And soon, the gold, silver, fine clothes, plentiful food, horses and donkeys would all be shared with the unknowing inhabitants of Samaria. Ironic, wasn't it, that liberty was discovered by lepers? God used the wounded to find the wealth.

The Grace That Can Happen

Leprosy kills, just as sin kills. Leprosy paralyzes, just as sin numbs the conscience. Jesus stared the lonely figure of death in the face. The gaunt face of evil, its beady eyes cloaked in a voluminous hood and its gaze hollow, could not diminish the Savior's desire to carry the weight of sin. Jesus took the skin ulcers, the gangrene of iniquity, and the paralysis of fear upon His own body. He adopted both the physical sores of leprosy and the spiritual sores of sin, and carried them in His own body to the cross.

I am that leper He led to a feast of grace. And I have come to your Samaria to give you the good news: Liberty is here! The table is set and the food is plentiful. There is no need to starve in the deserts of grief anymore. Your wounds can lead you to a place of worship. All you have to do is rise, like the four lepers, and move forward.

Remember, when the lepers arrived, the Syrians had vanished. God had already removed the slave masters. Likewise, Jesus has already removed sin and the binding elements of perversion. All you need to do is take the necessary steps forward to discover a camp overflowing with blessings and joy.

The Pain of Leprosy

Leprosy starts as a small spot. Something insignificant

turns into something worse, which, in turn, becomes the nightmare that was never dreamed, the sickness never imagined, and the pain never before endured.

That is the way sin is. It starts out as just a spot of curiosity and then eventually leads to scabs of regret. Before you know it, your whole body is subject to the leprosy of pride, lust, and self-indulgence. You start by thinking you can control a onetime deviation from the norm, but then transmigration takes place and you become the very thing you hated. You lose self-respect and, before long, you lose sight of the important things in life. Becoming distorted in your vision of grace, you begin thinking that life is just an opportunity to taste the forbidden, and you forget the way of the faithful.

Leprosy is not a minor problem like a headache that can be relieved by just popping a couple of aspirins. It's not like a toothache (although, admittedly, a toothache can be excruciating, especially if you need a root canal for an abscessed tooth). But even with an abscess, with a little dental attention — some drilling here and pain medication there – the problem is solved. But leprosy is different. Not only is it emotionally draining and socially humiliating, it's actually life-threatening. And it promises a slow, painful death.

Sin, like leprosy, is not something to be treated lightly — like marking the wrong answer on a test, or missing a turn a long journey, or bumping into someone at the store, knocking them down. Sin is serious. Sin is deadly. Sin is life-threateningly eternal.

Leprosy shoves its victims toward the walls of isolation. Lepers cannot just stroll down the neighborhood sidewalk, or sit at a coffee house enjoying a latte. They cannot stop by the park and swing with the kids, or throw a ball around with their buddies, or go shopping at the mall. They cannot go about life as if nothing is wrong, because when they're afflicted with leprosy, the sky has fallen, and the world they've known has come to an end. The leper will spend the rest of his days in a colony, which is stigmatized by the world as a place for dying without dignity.

Similarly, sin drives a sinner deeper and deeper within the walls of shame. The stronger the influence of certain sins in a man's life, the more private he becomes in his quest for denial, for justification, for a state of mind that is guilt-free and clean. So he hides. Such was the reaction of Adam and Eve in the garden. When they ate the forbidden fruit and stepped into the realm of revelation, they suddenly realized that their nakedness was shameful. They wanted to hide it, to get rid of it as soon as possible, to sew fig leaves together and create a form of salvation. Even though the salvation was self-made, they comforted themselves in their sin's hidden state. It wasn't until the voice of God spoke in the cool of the evening that they realized their self-made salvation would not work. Conviction blew in like a cyclone across the waters of their conscience.

They knew God's holy nature was not pleased with their hiding, yet hiding was the instinctive thing to do. For the leprosy of sin drives a man to a place of isolation from God, toward a colony of like-minded promise-breakers, to feel better about himself. It's just like a drunk who searches for other drunks in a bar to throw his arms around, and in the shared companionship of failure, laughs and laments over their common grievances.

In Adam and Eve's case, they were befriended by a serpent. It's hard to believe that before the bite of fruit, they lived in the blessed company of the Almighty. But after the bite, they degraded themselves by keeping company with a nefarious liar, one who loathed the goodness of both God and man. They petted a snake because the venom of deception was in their veins, the serum of independence and human aggrandizement had poisoned them. Their drinking buddy became public enemy number one — Lucifer.

They served the Lord one day, and Lucifer the next. That's like trading gold for dust, silver for unsavory salt. They walked away from the One who brought them joy, whose presence engendered virtue, and the intimacy that promised eternal regeneration and an unblemished physique. And for what? A guilt-stained existence, a death trap of temptation, and a failing body suddenly subject to pimples and wrinkles, aching joints and jaundice. And leprosy.

A man may hide behind a mask, but he can never fool God. God's light is too bright, too discerning; for He knows the intents of the heart. He knows our motives before we even act. Every thought that is stimulated by a desire to appease the flesh, and not the spirit, is already revealed to the master of the universe.

Sometimes a man searches for answers that make him feel better about what he is doing, rather than who he is. We seek justification, when we ought to seek transformation. We seek approval, when we ought to seek evolution. We want God to pat us on the back and pardon us, when the higher order would be a baptism of fire and a purging of baggage that robs us of our full potential.

Instead of looking for an excuse to exempt ourselves from guilt, we should concentrate on exposing ourselves to the light so that we might examine ourselves honestly. Only then will we walk away with a deeper appreciation for the grace of God. For that grace will lead us away from human limitation toward divine liberty, and on to infinite possibility, maturity and authority.

Chapter Two

Don't Just Gaze—Go!

In Genesis 13, we have the story of Abraham and Lot's separation. Strife between the herdsmen dictated a much-needed meeting between uncle and nephew. After some discussion, Abraham, being the congenial man that he was, pointed in a sweeping motion toward the expanse of land before them and encouraged Lot to take first pick. Abraham convinced Lot that separating the groups would relieve the tension between them, as the continued expansion of each man's flock was straining the relationship.

Lot scanned the fertile valleys, greedily examining the towns of Sodom and Gomorrah on the horizon. He decided to claim the plain of Jordan, replete with rich soil, sparkling streams, and abounding wildlife. Lot hugged his uncle, packed his bags, and left for the promises of happiness in the East.

Abraham gazed with great affection on his impulsive nephew as he departed. As his eyes brimmed with tears, and a thousand memories were recalled, Abraham heard the voice of the Lord:

Lift up now thine eyes, and look from the place where thou art northward, and southward, and eastward, and westward: For all the land which

*thou seest, to thee will I give it, and to thy seed for
ever. And I will make thy seed as the dust of the
earth: so that if a man can number the dust of the
earth, then shall thy seed also be numbered* (Genesis
13:14-16).

At this time of difficult family separation, Abraham,
received a great promise from the Lord. Although Lot
had chosen first, God had reserved the best for the "father of faith." Lot acted on what he saw, while Abraham,
as always, waited for what God said.

Abraham could look in every direction, as far as the
eye could see, and behold the everlasting boundaries of
God's promised provisions. He could see the land of destiny that would, one day, hold the countless inhabitants
of his seed. But Abraham was not just encouraged to
look:

*Arise, walk through the land in the length of it and in
the breadth of it; for I will give it unto thee* (v.17).

Abraham was not allowed to just gaze. *He was instructed to go.* We cannot merely *see* the good things of
God; we must *walk* in them. Beholding the promises of
God and behaving as joint-heirs of Christ are two totally
different things. We might see where we want to go, but
without active faith, that vision is nothing more than
virtual reality — a reality never realized because of inac-
tion. We cannot sit in our *Kadesh-barneas* (neutral
places) of life and boast about the land we own, while we
never move forward to actually possess what has been
given to us.

What good is a million dollars of inheritance money if we never go to the bank, withdraw it, and put that money to good use? It will merely gain interest for someone else's dreams. What good is a fertile field if we never plant seed in it? Only the weeds of wishful thinking will grow there.

To actually possess the blessings of God requires that we activate a proposed plan. The will of God also comes with a wheel of guidance, an accompanying desire that spurs us on to action. We cannot just sit by and watch God's blessings decay for lack of involvement. We must take initiative. The fulfillment of God's promises in our lives is usually reflective of the steps that we have taken. This is the true measure of attainment.

Don't just notice the beautiful orchard in your dreams — go forward, reach out, and with determination, you'll taste the nectar from its fruits. Don't just watch the train go by, lined with boxcars holding your hopes — get on board and follow the tracks of trust all the way to the blessings God has for you on the other side of the mountain.

Mere observers have to experience their ambitions vicariously, but obtainers seize the moment with hard work, discipline and tenacious faith. A joint-heir of Christ walks securely in the knowledge of his destiny and lives out in detail the meaning of that destiny, avoiding complacent reasoning that would immobilize godly principles and righteous living.

For Jehovah God is our Light and our Protector. He gives us grace and glory. No good thing will he withhold from those who walk along his paths (Psalm 84:11, TLB).

Walking Through

*Yea, though I walk through the valley of the shadow
of death, I will fear no evil: for thou art with me; thy
rod and thy staff they comfort me* (Psalm 23:4).

I believe the key to this verse is the words "I walk
through." The psalmist did not stand still, fearful, but he
moved forward. Step by step, he walked ahead. He did
not linger in the shadows — the sorrow that accompa-
nies disappointment and the grief that can hinder future
actions. Instead, he focused on the rod and staff of the
Shepherd and gradually inched his way out of danger.

If I dwell in self-pity long enough, gloom can take up
permanent residence in my heart. But I can trade in
gloom for gladness when I resolve to get on with life.
When I refuse to settle in the land of sorrow, God will
lead me on to greener pastures and emotional rest.

In Acts 28, Paul endured a shipwreck with a measure
of calm because he knew his divine destiny was to one
day stand before Caesar. He believed he wouldn't drown
because God still had plans for his life. So Paul walked
through....

In Samuel 17, David confidently faced Goliath, who
was armored with 450 pounds of brass, highly trained
for war, and undefeated in battle. But how could David
be eliminated by the heathen when he had been
anointed by heaven? David's destiny was to become
King of Israel, and at this point in life, he was still a
shepherd boy. So David walked through....

When faced with daunting tasks, fears, and insecurities from failed relationships, don't stand there gazing at
the shadows of defeat and death. Go forward in the confidence of God's love. Don't just gaze — go!

Walking Thrilled

For ye shall go out with joy, and be led forth with peace: the mountains and the hills shall break forth before you into singing, and all the trees of the field shall clap their hands. Instead of the thorn shall come up the fir tree, and instead of the brier shall come up the myrtle tree: and it shall be to the LORD for a name, for an everlasting sign that shall not be cut off (Isaiah 55:12).

This reference tells how Israel would leave the captivity in Babylon. They would leave with joy. No more sadness, waiting for sunshine moments in a cloudy world. No more chains, but real change.

You may think that a river of tears is the only river you will ever know; that being hurt by trusted friends is the only path you will ever walk. But take heart in this verse. Your impossibility zone is about to turn into a path of freedom.

If you have been captive to depression, unable to smile, incapable of energetic activity, look to Jesus. Not only will He take you through, He will make you joyful again. Your feelings of sorrow will be exchanged for the fountains of celebration.

Instead of the thorn, the fir tree will grow. Maybe you have gotten used to thorns — prickly trials that don't seem to go away. Just as a thorn is untouchable, so your unfulfilled dreams may have caused you pain, rather than joy. But God said the thorn would be replaced by the fir tree.

Fir trees were used to build the temple of God. So take comfort in this: God may use the thorns to build your faith through trials, but He'll use the fir tree to build His temple. The trial you're experiencing won't last forever because God does not dwell in the trial, but in you, His temple. Your pain will end, traded for the joy of true liberty. So, go forward!

Don't just gaze at the wilderness of your circumstances. Rise up and go. Your difficult journey of thorns is about to be transformed into the joyous fulfillment of your dreams. But you will never reach that place unless you advance.

Don't just gaze—go!

Trials - you can't go over them, you can't go under them, you have to go through them.
Sam- Thoughts
5/23/08

Chapter Three

The Splitting of Identities

Atomic energy. It is amazing in demonstration — the sheer force of science...the fission of a nucleus. The splitting of the atomic nucleus is what causes enormous energy to be released. This energy is the devastating power that can wipe out an entire city. This force is a dangerous weapon in the arsenal of any army with its mushrooming clouds, columns of energy rising at 360 feet per second, boiling curtains of radioactive vapor, licking flames and orange death. It is a scrolling chapter of chastisement in the annals of conflict.

On August 6, 1945, an atomic bomb named "Little Boy" was dropped on the unsuspecting inhabitants of Hiroshima. This uranium nightmare weighed four and one-half tons. The target, designated as the Aioi bridge, was missed by only 800 feet. In a flash of atomic fury, 66,000 people were killed. Just three days later, a plutonium instrument of death, named "Fat Man," was dropped on Nagasaki. In a split second the population of Nagasaki dropped from 422,000 to 383,000. Everything within a quarter mile radius was vaporized. Everything flammable within two miles burned. And the stirring conclusion of this display of atomic power was that the bombs utilized only 1/10th of 1 percent of their respective explosive capabilities.

Similarly, until we separate our fears from our faith, we are only using a meager portion of God's power available to us. Until we separate ourselves from the indulgences of the world, our capabilities as disciples will be diminished. Until we have fission in the body of Christ that frees us from petty jealousies and ministerial malice, we will continue to be frustrated by the level of return that we are receiving from such a high-priced commodity. When God has equipped us to change the world, and we are still outnumbered by the followers of Eastern religions, are we really living up to our respective explosive capabilities? After all, we were paid for by the blood of the Lamb — that makes the Church the most important purchase of all time. So how can we live up to the expectations of God?

Great Power

In the spiritual sense, it is the splitting of the Adam that brings great power. Jesus was the second Adam. The book of Hebrews tells us that He was the veil of the temple. His flesh torn for the salvation of sinners is analogous to the tearing of this veil. During the final moments of Christ's suffering, the clouds coiled in anger, the ground shook in trembling respect, and electrical currents shot through the blackened sky.

The angels held their fluttering wings as the Lamb drew His final breaths. Jesus, now at the summit of salvation, now at the peak of prophetic significance, uttered His last statement: "It is finished." His head dropped; His body sagged. The cross creaked under the full weight of the dead Prince of Peace. And somewhere in the distance, beyond the gate of the temple, past the brazen glare of the altar, the gurgling waters of the laver, the court of the Gentiles and the statuesque altar of incense, was a tearing sound. The veil that separated ordinary man from the Shekinah glory was torn in half. From top to bottom, this rough ripping of fabric, this splitting of the elegant tapestries echoed through the halls of eternity.

This was the splitting of the second Adam. It would soon cause a chain reaction of apostolic revival that is still affecting the world today with explosions of holiness, flames of faith, and mushrooming manifestations of healing ministries incinerating our fears. These are the things that happen when the Adam is split.

When we split the carnal from the spiritual, there is going to be fallout. Cynical members will be at war with sensitive saints. A fission of fear from faith can be the start of a chain reaction that leads to miracles. It takes faith to please God, and the more division there is between human fear and heavenly understanding, the more powerful our churches will become. The more faith we exhibit, the more God reveals Himself. The more God reveals Himself, the greater the light of liberty and power.

Revival Power

Revival becomes explosive in nature when the carnal mind is separated from the spiritual mind. The carnal mind uses reasoning, doubt, and the intellect to block divine intentions. But the spiritual mind opens the door to the demonstration of God's presence, unhindered by cynicism. This is why we must be careful what side of the division we find ourselves on. If we are on the side of carnal indifference to the Word of God, then it may be the detonation of judgment that vaporizes the reprobate heart from the congregation of the righteous. But separating ourselves from our fears and clinging to the righteousness of God creates the impetus for His inspiration. He will empower us to accomplish great things, unhindered by the boundaries of unbelief.

In the same way that nuclear power is derived from the splitting of atomic nuclei, so the Church obtains power when it separates from the world. When the elements of hedonism are divided from heart of Christianity, we gain strength. The catalyst for this is the cross. Jesus said, "If any man will come after Me, let him take up his cross and follow Me." We must desire to model ourselves after Christ's character if we are to be effective in the war for souls.

You will find that those who are desperate for a move of God are often the ones who are willing to deny themselves. They are sold out to God. They are not afraid to give everything for the cause of the Kingdom. These people become the catalyst for God's covenant. They illuminate Scriptures that speak of what is dead in the Church, what has become lethargic, or what has been dulled by defilement. These believers pray intensely. They are the movers and shakers in the house of God. They are not the silent majority but are the shouting magistrates of divine purpose.

I remember preaching a revival message at a church one time that seemed to be stuck in a state of apathy.

Their level of excitement about the topic was about as high as a lecture on grave-digging might arouse at a cemetery convention. In other words, there was very little enthusiasm for the subject. Even their clapping was robotic and formal.

After enduring several nights of this, I decided to search for one person in the congregation who might be a stimulus for change. I found him. He was a young man who truly hungered for the things of God. He was tired of placid services, and his heart stirred for the mighty winds of revival. Once I sensed his desire, I began to focus my attention on him during the messages. It wasn't long before he was praying with people at the altar, teaching home Bible studies, and initiating praise in the services. He became a catalyst for revival. His activities then spawned a hunger in others to get involved. The church took on a new identity. It was no longer a desert of parched parishioners enduring another dry service, but it became a river of strength and motivation for the whole region.

The book of Hebrews tells us that

The word of God is sharper than any two-edged sword, piercing even to the dividing asunder of soul and spirit, of the joints and marrow, and is a discerner of the thoughts and intents of the heart.

The word "dividing" means "to separate or distribute." In this passage, the contextual meaning has to do with the power of God's Word to give or take life. His Word can sever the connection between the sensual, mortal part of man and the eternal soul of man. He can divide the temporary from the eternal. He can separate the physical body of flesh and muscle from the eternal blueprint that is the soul.

This verse cuts to the very core of a person's intellect, passions and ambitions. The Word of God can perceive the secrets of a man's soul. It can separate his motives from his actions. It perceives patterns of behavior that stem from a sinful environment or orientation.

There is separation of content. The meaning of life is changed when there is a splitting of identities. You cease to live for temporal things and reach for the next revelation of God's character, as opposed to the next wrung on the ladder of success. Having fruits of integrity means more than an orchard of worldly riches. The heart is filled with the reality of God's love and not the fantasies of short-lived affections. You find in the heart of the man who has split from worldly needs the explosive qualities that can bring heathen nations to their knees.

Jesus said that out of the abundance of the heart the mouth speaketh. If the chambers of your soul were open to investigation, what would be found there? Would there be sadness, which comes out in negative ways of speaking? Would there be sins against God, which are revealed in words of defiance? Think of what must have been in the heart of Judas. What signs of corruption must have been present in the secret recesses of his heart? Could it have been the rust of rebellion, the debris of lies and self-justification, the high-backed throne of greed?

The contents of a servant's heart are altogether different. There you will find the emblems of suffering, a cross on which he daily crucifies the lust of the flesh, a few nails with which he fastens sacrifice of his will, and a crown of thorns placed on his mental brow to keep his thoughts free of pride.

When one's heart is right, the need to be recognized is subverted by the greater need to be intimate with God. The temptations of fame and fortune take a backseat to unwavering faith in God. And this driving passion is second to none in the race toward eternity.

Such was the case with the Apostle Paul. "For me to live is Christ, for me to die is gain." His every heartbeat was a pulsation of devotion to God. He did not live to fill his belly with the delicacies of political tables. He did not pretend to be compassionate so he could manipulate others. The silver of his character did not tarnish in the face of dignitaries, but he gleamed with all the polished power of truth. He used his education as a tool, not a treasure. He did not seek personal gain, but he lived for God's grace.

And truly he turned the Gentile world upside down!

Chapter Four

From Migron to Miracle

In the land of Gibeah, an interesting sequence of events proved to be a lesson in bravery and reliability. Shadows played on the rolling hills as the sun peeked through the velvety clouds gliding in the steady winds of mid-summer. The high country hinted at approaching storms as gentle thunder rumbled beyond the shoulders of the highest mountains. A Philistine garrison resided covertly among nature's rocky fortresses; mysterious trails leading to their adversaries were sprinkled lightly with whitened sage. At times a hint of rain, blended with the mint-like scent of the sage, created a strange perfume in the air. But on this day, the coppery scent of blood would also fill the air.

King Saul sat under a pomegranate tree in Migron, his gaunt face and restless eyes studying the horizon as if searching for battle strategies in the stars. (This pomegranate tree was most likely the rock of Rimmon mentioned in Judges 20:45, rather than a literal pomegranate tree.) It is possible that Saul suffered with a Migron headache, not knowing what his next move should be. Migron was a Hebrew term derived from the root words "terror" and "cast down." We all have suffered from spiritual Migron headaches, unable to think clearly because our minds are weighted down with fear.

There was a large cave in this area, and Saul's 600 soldiers found safe lodging for rest and recuperation. They sat around small fires yawning, stretching, and sharpening their spears with flint, sending sparks into the unlit tunnels of the cave. They roasted wild boar on spits and ate ravenously in preparation for battle. Some soldiers futilely attempted to clean blood droplets off their sandals, while others polished shields with fresh olive oil — to prevent them from cracking in the arid climate, and also to consecrate the shields to God.

A few chosen men walked around the camp and checked the instruments of war, insuring every man's readiness and protection. Weapons were few among the Israelites, due to the lack of well-trained blacksmiths, so the skirmishes with the Philistines had to be fought carefully and with strategic precision.

Jonathan, King Saul's son, left his father sitting under the pomegranate tree. He ordered his armor bearer to accompany him to observe, and possibly attack, the arrogant garrison of the Philistines. In a courageous plot, Jonathan left the camp of safety for the wilderness of danger, knowing very well that he might die. But he knew he had to go. Someone had to take a stand against the intimidating forces of Philistia. Someone had to leave the entrapment of terror in the caves of Migron and face the enemy. The heathens from the west had wearied them long enough, and Jonathan wanted to prove himself valiant.

Godly Infiltration

It is one thing to sit safely with others and boast about one's bravery, but it's something altogether different to stand face-to-face with the enemy. The boldness of Christians is put to the test not in safe circles of praise, but in the streets of resistance, where the majority fight God's Word. For the Christian, one's bravery is measured by the steps of faith taken beyond the warm fellowship of like-minded believers, into the cold world of atheism and hedonism. There, one truly becomes a witness, to proclaim the "acceptable year of the Lord."

At this point in the story, Jonathan did not know whether he would survive his mission. But the sheer impossibility of obtaining freedom drove him onward. Jonathan and his armor bearer walked carefully, mindful of Philistine scouts in the area. They came to a peculiar-looking valley surrounded by two rocky pillars. One pillar, named *Bozez* (which means "shining," due to its chalky appearance), stood tall, its conical form facing the village of Michmash to the north. The other pillar, named *Seneh* (which means "thorn," probably from a lone acacia tree on its top), towered in alignment with the small village of Geba to the south. Buzzards circled above, as if aware that a generous meal might be imminent.

The wind shifted from west to south, almost like a spiritual indicator of changes coming in the battle. As the armor bearer scanned every angle, examining different routes to approach the enemy post, Jonathan suddenly narrowed his eyes in discernment and proposed a spiritual plan.

Let's cross over to the camp of those heathen

*Philistines. Maybe, the Lord will help us; if He does,
nothing can keep Him from giving us the victory, no
matter how few of us there are.*

The young armor bearer smiled perceptively and
said with militant resolve, "Whatever you want to do, I
am with you."

*All right, we will go across and let the Philistines see
us. If they tell us to wait for them to come to us, then
we will stay where we are. But if they tell us to go to
them, then we will, because that will be the sign that
the Lord has given us victory over them* (I Samuel
14:8 TEV).

God's Involvement

Jonathan included God in the process. *Victories are
easier to obtain if God is a part of the plan.* I have entered many difficult situations to find that with God present in the decision-making, those difficulties can be
minimized. The fields of struggle yield much more
quickly when the seed of God's Word is planted and the
principles of truth are followed. Likewise, Jonathan realized that military training alone wasn't enough to tackle
a dangerous mission. He wanted God's assurance, God's
directive. How many times do we falter against the
enemy because we try to do it our way, without first
considering the way of God?

Jonathan also understood that when God was present, that made a majority. Although they might be
physically outnumbered, if God was there, they would
triumph. Glory would come to Him. God does not work
by human standards of measurement. What we might

call a pint of potential, God may call a gallon of power. It is part of the human dilemma that we see things from a pessimistic perspective. But God added to any equation transforms the powerless into the preeminent.

Isaiah 55:9 states,

For as the heavens are higher than the earth, so are my ways higher than your ways, and my thoughts than your thoughts.

Higher, here, means "to soar, to be lofty, to be exalted." God sees things from a different vantage point than we do. He sees the proverbial "big picture." He is not limited by differing opinions, past failures that bring future fears, or rivers of sorrow that envelop the heart. There is nothing that obstructs God's view as He looks down on us from above. He knows that nothing is impossible. He has supernatural leverage, whereas we have carnal limitations. We say the sky is the limit; but with God, not even the sky can limit Him.

Possibly the Philistine garrison thought these Israelite soldiers were deserters. So they called to them, "Come up here, we have something to tell you!"

At this point, Jonathan knew that God favored the Israelites. So he spoke confidently: "Follow me, the Lord has given us victory over them." He made a faith announcement prior to the engagement.

Faith calls the outcome according to God's involvement, while man's philosophy calls it according to educational evolvement. It is normal to measure an army's chances of success by observing the technological advances, information, inventory of weapons and military prowess of the enemy. But the child of God must primarily discern the purpose of God. Human intelligence may win a battle, but heavenly intervention will always win the war.

God's participation can spare us sorrow's precipitation. An alliance with God can keep us safe from compromising relationships. It will help us avoid partnerships with marketing wolves who merely seek to exploit anointing for monetary gain.

Psalm 20:7 declares,

> *Some trust in chariots, and some in horses, but we will remember the name of the Lord our God.*

Grace Invasion

Suddenly Jonathan's countenance changed. His eyes looked like pools of black oil set ablaze. His jaw thrust forward defiantly. He quickly climbed upward as his armor bearer followed him. At the top, they confronted the enemy. They were like members of a football team, barreling through the garrison as a fullback plows through the defending team, making a way for a running back. Jonathan collided with each Philistine soldier, grunting with fierce initiative, tumbling the enemy to the ground in defeat. The heavy armor of the Philistine soldiers clanked against the rocks, helmets popped off and rolled down the hill, and swords stuck in the ground, vibrating momentarily from the sudden impact.

The armor bearer finished off each fallen soldier with a swift stab of his knife. Blood ran down the narrow path, a stream of red that branched into several tributaries. Nearby rocks were soaked in the crimson evidence of the enemy's death. Soaring vultures squawked in anticipation of a fleshly feast. At times Jonathan felt a stabbing pain in his shoulder, but the intensity of the mission and the adrenaline of the moment served to temporarily dull the pain.

Jonathan and his armor bearer proved to be a duet of destruction, composing a song of perdition for the proud heathens and oppressors of Israel. When it was all over, 20 Philistines were killed. The soldiers had hurled insulting remarks at Jonathan and his armor bearer, but soon the winds carried their howls and dying whispers to the caverns of hell. While moments earlier they had swaggered proudly over the lowly Israelites, now they lay motionless in the sand, eyes expressionless, mouths silent.

This act of selfless courage displayed by Jonathan and his armor bearer changed the emotional atmosphere of the conflict. From that moment on, the Philistine armies trembled in fear before the Israelites. This is also what takes place when the garrisons of evil stand against the people of God. Spirits of condemnation may hurl insults against righteousness, but if the people of God stand together, pray together, work together, and go forward with spiritual purpose, the enemies of faith will mourn in defeat.

Jonathan's name means "Jehovah has given." God's gift to our current generation, which quakes in abject fear of terrorism, an uncertain economy, and escalating violence, is a love-bearing Church willing to combat the tyrannical forces of darkness. The Church of the living God is intended to be a refuge for the weary, a group of special forces trained in compassion for the hurting, ready to attack depression and loneliness. I pray daily for a chance to make a difference to someone living in the caves of trepidation, unable to enjoy the goodness of

God because they are blinded by past failures and present insecurities.

James 1:17 states,

> *Every good gift and every perfect gift is from above, and cometh down from the Father of lights, with whom is no variableness, neither shadow of turning.*

When the moon eclipses the sun, a great shadow falls on the earth. The heavenly bodies are subject to the varying degrees of universal alignments and movements. But with God, there is no shadow of change. His light is eternally fixed. He will always be there for the contrite soul who cries out to Him. His gifts and goodness are not subject to the laws of sin and corruption. In a world of much anxiety, this is a calming assurance. God does not change. He chooses to love, and although His operations seem at times mysterious and beyond our understanding, I have complete trust that, whether in life or death, He will not fail me.

In the end, Jonathan and his armor bearer proved that just sitting in Migron (terror and depression) will not bring the victory. They stepped forward, took a leap of faith, and God rewarded their action with a miraculous outcome.

You don't have to stay in the cave of defeat, convinced that hiding is better than having. Step out of your cave. Better yet, step out with a prayer partner. There's no telling what garrison of hell you may conquer in the most impossible time and in the most impossible way.

Chapter Five

Follow the Instructions

Recently I put together a basketball goal for my son, Adrian. As usual, I attempted to assemble the parts without first reading the instructions. Somewhere, buried deep in the self-sufficient recesses of my mind, exists a frustration factory. Every time I try to construct something without consulting the manual, the project doesn't turn out well. Boxes of aggravation are piled on my desk. What am I supposed to do with all this wasted time? I'm ready to fire that factory manager. Oh, wait — it's me.

Picture the scene. A hammer, screws, bolts, nuts, poles, brackets, ratchets, screwdrivers, a basketball rim, and a base all await my ingenious hands. Now, the temperature outside is just cool enough to be enjoyable if I pull off the miracle of first-time completion. But it can also be irritatingly hot when my blood pressure soars because of having to start over. Move over, Mt. Saint Helens — the "expert" put the wrong bracket in the wrong place. Now, if I were creating an artistic masterpiece, prized for its design eccentricities, I'd be on my way to New York to sign a multimillion-dollar contract. But, it's just a basketball goal, begging to be put together correctly.

I was amazed by the brilliance of the person who wrote the instructions. Unlike me, they had put many of these same models together. Once I followed the instructions, carefully examining the illustrations, numbering my parts, and laying out my pieces, the riddle of the basketball goal was not impossible to figure out. And no, there was not a secret conspiracy within Huff Industries (the maker of the basketball goal) to seek me out and drive me insane with a baffling set of plans. Now, the finished product sits in the driveway — something even Michael Jordan would be proud of.

I have learned, from many experiences with a hammer and a long list of projects, that you *can* start over. New beginnings are as easy as returning to the instructions to find out what's wrong. In the same way, we are taught, at an early age, that there is a right way and a wrong way to do things. This is true in many areas of life: education, sports, business and even marriage.

Study to shew thyself approved unto God, a workman that needeth not to be ashamed, rightly dividing the word of truth (II Timothy 2:15).

The basic meaning of this passage is to do it right. Careful observation makes for correct application. You can't randomly flip through the Bible, read about a few interesting topics, and expect to completely grasp the depth of the Scriptures. It takes seasons of patience, years of passionate probing to really understand both the meaning and the Author. It demands relationship, and relationships are not forged overnight. They take time to pursue and develop. What marriage proves its mettle in a couple of years? But examine a faithful couple like the Hatchers, who have been married for 70 years, and you'll get a glimpse of what it means to do it right.

The Hatchers work as assistant pastors at Landmark Tabernacle in Denver. The gray-haired couple has been faithfully doing God's work for more than 50 years. She makes a delicious walnut pie, and he is quick to tell you, "Jesus Christ is the same yesterday, today and forever." Their affectionate banter entertains and softens the heart. Their steps lag with age, but their spiritual vigor remains strong.

Do they have arguments? Absolutely. Did they ever feel like giving up? Amen. But they studied each other. They learned the patterns of love that work, the undying formulas of commitment that can fix any hurt or any misunderstanding. They worked diligently, by the grace and help of God, to let compatibility blossom and trust deepen, to endure storms, and to remain in love. If staying together truly causes each spouse to favor the other, then the Hatchers are twins. Seventy years of marriage defies the logic of our generation, as folks are treating marriage with the same regard as a five-year loan: once the thrills are paid off, it's time to find a new love. How did the Hatchers do it? When things seemed impossible, they followed the instructions. They trusted the Word of God.

When temptation comes, we should not try to stumble our way through it, blindly trusting our instincts. We should not try to drum up a clever justification but rather, we need to go back to the instructions and find out how to defeat the peddlers of perversion, the solicitors of sin, and the vendors of vindictiveness. "Thy word is a lamp unto my feet, and a light unto my path" (Psalm 119:105).

A Safe Guide

The instructions of God guide us safely through unknown lands. By reflecting on Scripture, we are able to detect the hidden pitfalls of self-expression, dangerous ledges of pride, or treacherous paths of desire. Potentially bewildering journeys can be mapped out beforehand, saving us heartache and worry.

Dangers perpetually lurk in the carnal heart, and slight detours from the truth can bring devouring guilt and shame. But if we keep God's teachings, we can eliminate frustrations that stem from confusion. As in the example of the basketball goal, much time was wasted doing it my way. Once I returned to the guide, I not only put it together right, but I saved myself continued delays in progress. How many blessings of God do we miss or arrive at late because we simply fail to follow directions? I know: talk is cheap. But talk turned into action is invaluable.

It is sometimes difficult to admit we have done something wrong. Better to leave it and move on, we think. But eventually, our sins will catch up to us. And then we'll have to undo the mistakes, much like trying to untie shoelaces that have become knotted up.

Often, the impossibility zone is really a place of pride. When we are finally willing to walk away from our narcissism, our belief that we know best, then we'll begin to see the thick fog hiding our miracle begin to lift. We'll see it God's way. We'll do it God's way. And all of a sudden, things are not as difficult as they once seemed.

Are you ready to escape the darkness of disappointment? Are you tired of trying to do things your way, with frustrating results? Pick up the Word of God. Read His instructions. Your life is a mixture of successes and failures, and God has a reason for every part of it. Even our trials have a purpose. Ephesians 2 tells us we are "fitly framed together" (v. 21).

Every piece of your life has a purpose. Let God help you construct it correctly. Follow His instructions.

Chapter Six

Stop the Funeral
(Luke 7:11-16)

Black clouds hung low over the mountains, appearing as if cooked in an oven of sorrow. Rhythmic droppings of rain fell in the foothills and threatened to come closer to the city, but the sun shone in defiance on the opposite horizon. For one woman, the world stood still that day.

Just within the city of Nain, a funeral procession was in progress. A wooden coffin, shouldered by several men, commanded the center of a path leading out of the city gate. A widow paced along wearily, leaning on the arms of her closest friends. She mourned for her only son, now tucked away in the box of death. Soon he would be planted in the ground, a human seed of memory.

The widow's joy had withered and tears of pain now rained on the barren soil of her life. She had lost both a husband and now her only son. No doubt, she felt guilty as a mother and as a wife, wondering what she could have done differently to save them. The sounds of thunder in the distant hills synchronized with the crushing loneliness that stormed in her heart.

According to Jewish custom, a body must be buried within 24 hours of death. Hours earlier, the son's mother was by his bedside when he drew his last breath. With tears rolling down her cheeks, onto her dead son's face, she reached out to close his eyes one final time. His jaws were bound shut with a napkin, and his body was wrapped in strips of linen. The mother's shrill cry of lamentation had announced to the world that her son was dead.

She groaned in agony, stooped low to the ground, grabbed a handful of dirt and tossed it to the winds. Others followed her example, creating a small dust storm that blew away from the crowd. The angle of the afternoon sun stretched an eerie shadow of the coffin over the vine-laden path. With each step, the mother drew closer to entering a cavern of despair from which she might never find her way out.

Possibly after this mournful occasion, she intended to lock herself away and become a depressed recluse for the rest of her life. She may have believed that the remainder of her days would be filled with restless nights, painful memories, and wishful thinking. She would sit in the unlit corners of her empty house and drink wine until her sorrows were dulled, mumbling about the good days when her husband and son were alive.

No one can really predict how an individual will react to grief. Some rise out of it quickly and move on with life, making new friends and helping others cope with their own losses. Others bury themselves with the dead and merely exist in a robotic state until death comes at its appointed hour.

In the story, Jesus noticed the somber crowd

weaving its way to the gravesite. He walked past the huddled mourners until He reached the coffin. Soon, the rays of Jesus' resurrection power fell on the group, bringing gasps of amazement and newfound joy.

For the dead boy's lungs suddenly expanded with air once again. With a gasp, his breath blew against the wooden lid. Blood circulated and his heart pounded against his rib cage with renewed vigor. His lips, once painted gray by the grim reaper, were now painted red again by the Word of life, and his pale skin regained its former tanned glow. The shadow of death slunk away. The worms of the nether regions took their appetite for dead flesh to another place. The sprawling trees nestled on the morbid hillside where the boy was to be buried would have to shade his grave another day.

A lonely mother was given a son to love a second time. Gleefully, she grabbed her son, covering his face with joyful kisses. With eyes gleaming with renewed energy, eyes that moments earlier had been unplugged from hope, she turned and thanked the Messiah repeatedly.

In the same way that Jesus stepped in to stop a literal funeral, He wants to stop a funeral that you might be experiencing in your heart. Maybe the thing that you've buried is an area of faith. If so, this story has tremendous spiritual implications for you.

Stop the funeral! It is not time to die
    in your desert of grief.
Stop the funeral! Your heart is not beyond repair.
Stop the funeral! The coffin of your failure needs to be
    traded in for a cache of fruit — the fruit of love after

brokenness, joy after trauma, and peace after pain.

Stop the funeral! Bypass the burial grounds of self-pity, bitterness, and anger.

Stop the funeral! Feel the Master's hand touch your deadened faith and raise it back to life for the Kingdom of God.

Stop the funeral! Doubt should not bury you in the field of failure.

Stop the funeral! Compromise for a moment should not put you six feet under in the grounds of forgotten convictions.

Stop the funeral! Don't let the rigor mortis of religion be the last movement of your faith. You don't have to be stiff with stubbornness. Don't let the your hand fly up in mocking praise because you've lost the light of truth and spiritual understanding.

Stop the funeral! An ancient burial ground of stones is known as a barrow. Don't let the enemy put you in a barrow of blame, where your hopes are covered with the stones of every mistake you've ever made.

Stop the funeral! Don't let darkness and deception spread the ashes of your trust over the seas of regret and despair. Rise up. Push off the lid. Get out of your coffin. Walk confidently again. Live again.

Stop the funeral! Don't live in the cemetery of sorrow. Don't let the enemy shovel the dirt of anguish on your grave. Rise up in the joy of the Lord. Allow God to spread a smile on your face.

Stop the funeral! Don't let Satan write your epitaph, using descriptive language that defines you as a failure.

Stop the funeral! Don't let rebellion take you to the

mortuary of mercy, where grace is unreachable and the call of God is forever lost.

Compassion's Dilemma

"And when the Lord saw her, he had compassion on her" (v.13). Jesus cannot hear the whimpers of a broken heart and just walk by, unmoved. His attention is drawn to those who are staggering in a storm of grief. Like a magnet, Jesus drew near this suffering woman. As Proverbs 18:24 says, Jesus is a friend that "sticketh closer than a brother." "Sticketh" is the Hebrew word *debeq* which means "to adhere, joining, and stick closer." When we feel crushed by sorrow, Christ comes close to us.

When we grieve in the midst of trauma and family loss, the grace giver speeds to the scene with affection and peace. Jesus adheres to us in our anguish until we come out with anointing. He sticks to us in our stress, until we come out stronger. He meshes with us in our misery, until we come out with new meaning. He hitches onto us in your hurt and pulls us out of the pit of despair. He embraces us in our brokenness.

Confrontational Deliverance

"And he came and touched the bier" (v.14). God cares about our pain. He's concerned about the struggling elements of the heart. His touch is not merely reserved for the perfected materials of the universe: "For we have not an high priest which cannot be touched by the infirmities of our flesh" (Hebrews 4:15). On this particular day, when many staggered toward the cemetery with broken hearts, Jesus gladly accepted the challenge to step forth and restore joy. He did it with action, not just soothing words.

In this generation of constant change, terrorist fears, and increased wars on democracy, God is raising up men and women who are unafraid of spiritual confrontation. They are armed with humility and persistent prayer. They live in the freedom of God's Kingdom, for where the Spirit of the Lord is, there is liberty. Chains of immorality cannot hold them down. Tyrants of deception are matchless against the righteous lovers of truth. And just as Jesus stepped forth to touch the bier, so these Christians of the end time are poised to confront death and hell in order to sustain, restore, and give life.

Concluding Declaration

"God has visited." This should be the heart cry of every Christian. Every corner of society should echo with amazement that God has visited them. When a poor man is given bread from the hand of a saint, let him say, "God has visited." When a suicidal teenager is detoured from death to a prayer meeting by a friend, let that person say, "God has visited." When a neighborhood experiences Christian charity in the midst of tragedy, let the hurting say, "God has visited." When the cancer patient feels the warm hand of an intercessor on his brow, and a miracle replaces his misery, let that person say, "God has visited." When a tearful mother stands over the casket of her slain son in battle, and she feels the gentle squeeze of a concerned pastor's hand, let her say, "God has visited."

Thinking Outside of the Box

In the story, everyone in the funeral procession had their minds in a box. They were thinking routine, sorrowful thoughts, shedding tears in a normal reaction to the fact that one had been taken at too young an age. The countenance of each person shuffling along spoke of shadows and dust, their cheeks sagging under the gravity of death. A cold body lay in the box. A widow's only son lay in the box. What should be their response? How should the bystanders, friends and neighbors act?

Then Jesus came along and interrupted the routine. He stepped into the midst of a normal custom — a funeral. A tragedy had befallen the mother. And yet, Jesus calmly walked over, touched the box with the dead boy in it, and turned a morbid moment into a miracle celebration. Why? Because Jesus thought outside of the box.

So the next time you are trapped in a box of dead faith, negative thinking, and skeptical vision, let the One who thinks outside of the box take over.

The beautiful thing about Jesus' actions was that He didn't patronize the grief-stricken people. He just focused on the power outside of the box — His Presence. And He delivered the one inside the box to join Him outside. So when the Lord steps into your dead situation, realize that He's not just trying to get you to *think* outside the box; He wants you to *live* outside the box. Otherwise, your religion just remains a dead routine on the way to the cemetery.

You can either think outside the box or stink inside the box. If you stay in the box of fear long enough, your faith will start decomposing and your attitude will stink of paranoia, lack of trust, cynicism, and pride. But if you let Jesus revive a dream that's dead in the box — dead from the disappointment of trying one thing after another — you will not only think outside of the box, you will truly live outside of the box.

So why not rise up today? Why not revisit a burial site of dreams and stand there with a fresh perception of God's sovereignty? Let Him empower your mind and heart to believe that on the barren grounds of past failure, a beautiful testimony can be birthed. Stop the funeral. Think outside of the box. Trade the coffin of isolation and fear for the cause of Christ — one that is alive, exciting, and faith-enriching.

Chapter Seven

Tear the Roof Off
(Luke 5:17-26)

The crowd pressed in to hear the Messiah teach, eager listeners pushing to the front, wide-eyed and anxious for a miracle. The soothing voice of Jesus drifted through the hot air, refreshing the ears of poor men and women with hope. Some leaned against the clay walls of the house, tingeing their sleeves with dust. Husbands used their wives as props, resting their hands upon their shoulders, studiously absorbing every parable and principle taught by Jesus.

Over in the corner, various scribes from the temple muttered occasionally about something the Teacher said, exchanging mocking glances with one another, shrugging their shoulders, extending their hands like confused children and just generally posing. You could distinguish them from the lowly publicans, for they were dressed in colorful silk garments and wore headpieces crafted by the best seamstress in town. They swaggered about, smirking, as if they were always ready to speak a wise word of correction to some infidel. They usually huddled together at every meeting Jesus conducted, like the defense on the opposing football team, ready to make a goal line stance against any spiritual teaching Jesus tried to put into the hungry hearts of the people. They despised His teaching, but they hated His healing power even more.

Outside the house, where the sun beat down and cooked the dry earth, four men shuffled along bearing the weight of their paralyzed friend on a cot. They were late for the meeting, and as they looked at the large crowd spilling out from every doorway and window, they knew it would be impossible to enter the house. They talked among themselves, debating whether to come back later, but finally resolved to do the only thing left that made sense — they would climb up onto the roof.

If the paralytic had been a renowned politician from the area or the son of someone famous, he no doubt would have been granted quick access to the front of the line, the crowd quickly parting to make way for him. But he wasn't a well-known person. He was just an ordinary man with an extraordinary problem.

Access to the house would not come easy. But his friends determined among themselves to do whatever it took to seize Christ's attention. (Aren't you glad access in the Kingdom of God is not based on your name, but on Jesus' name?)

As Jesus taught, a loud scraping noise caught the attention of the crowd. They looked up to see what was causing the commotion. It sounded like roofers were repairing a torn section of the roof. Maybe an army of rats was clawing at a secret entrance to what they believed to be a cheese factory. Or perhaps a flock of birds was scraping together materials from the owner's house to build a nest in some distant tree.

But the reality was even more startling. Four men were not repairing the roof — they were removing it. They stacked tiles in little mounds and pulled away bamboo and thatch, raining dust and debris on the bewildered multitude below. Warm rays of sun began to bathe the spectators. Some shaded their eyes from the luminous intrusion. Others no doubt shook their heads in disbelief and mumbled, "What insane asylum let these men free?"

"We could use a little more sun in this room," someone may have kidded.

"If they wanted a roofing job, this seems like a crazy way to let people know" retorted a wily old man.

Jesus stopped teaching and simply watched in amazement. Descending through the roof, dappled by sunrays and shadows, a cot holding a crippled man inched lower and lower until it touched the floor. The house seemed to change from a sanctuary to a circus. But this was not some act from Barnum & Bailey — this was a jaw-dropping, mesmerizing demonstration of love and faith.

The paralytic looked longingly in the direction of Jesus, his gaunt, pale face tilted upwards, pleading. His atrophied legs looked no thicker than wooden arrows. No doubt, the man had been flung from the bow of shame many times.

Jesus lovingly gazed up at the men and then at the paralytic. Warmed by their brave intrusion, he said with much compassion, "Son, your sins are forgiven."

The Pharisees grimaced as if each one had swallowed pigeon feathers. Their faces turned red with indignation as they loudly voiced objections to the Teacher's words.

"Why does this man speak blasphemies? Who can forgive sins but God?"

In response, the discerner of the thoughts and intents of the heart asked, "Is it easier to say to this paralyzed man, "Your sins are forgiven," or to say, "Get up, pick up your mat, and walk"? I will prove to you then that the Son of Man has authority on earth to forgive sins."

He turned to the paralytic, smiled at him, and said with resonant authority, "I tell you, get up, take up your mat, and go home!"

Electrical currents of sensation shot through the man's legs, and they jerked as spasms of healing brought life back to his dead nerves and feeble muscles. Perhaps he appeared a bit like a marionette bouncing on invisible strings. His eyes lit up with excitement, his face beaming with the brightest smile in years. He shoved himself upward, wobbled a moment or two on his repaired legs, stooped over, seized the bed that had carried him, and quickly walked away. He had entered the room propped up by four friends. Now, he left the room prancing like a little child who had just been given a lifetime supply of candy.

For awhile, even the critics were transformed into praisers. Although their amazement would soon shrink back into hateful cynicism, for now they glorified God. Even their ensuing comments were enthusiastic.

"We have seen strange things this day!"

Notice they did not say "supernatural," or "sovereign," but "strange." The word "strange" comes from the Greek word "paradoxa," meaning "contrary to expectation." A paradox: something that appears impossible, and yet is real. That's as far as these men would go in complimenting the work of God. Unlike the paralytic, who walked away carrying his symbol of despair, the Pharisees left the room still bound to their cots of contempt.

No Ceiling on Faith

What I find interesting about the active faith of the four friends is that they went to extremes for a miracle. Jesus, on the inside of the house, unreachable by normal means, represented the only hope of healing. He was the seed of restoration inside the clay shell of someone's home. They peeled away the roof, tearing off the exterior to experience a miracle moment. The lesson that these men help us learn is that *there is no ceiling on faith.*

You may be facing an impossible situation, such as a doctor's diagnosis of an incurable disease. These are the facts of your situation, but faith is not subject to fact; fact is subject to faith. Facts are not the "substance of things hoped for." Facts are merely statements of reality that are cold, hard, and without mystery. Faith, however, is the mystery of God's purpose at work; and what seems at first to be unchangeable is filtered through the power of God's Word. "Faith," as Hebrews states, "bears evidence of things not seen." This is the complete opposite of fact. Fact is based on analysis and documentation — that which is seen.

Don't let the facts of your past, cloud your faith for breakthroughs in the future. Whatever limitations you have put on yourself or perceptions of others that bind you, climb above them. Tear off the roof. Declare the testimony of Jesus to be true — the power to overcome death, hell, and the grave.

When the enemy tells you that finances will always be minimal, and your promotion will never come because you are undeserving, tear off the roof and put your faith in the presence of a caring Christ.

When condemnation haunts you, reminding you of past failures, present pain, and future consequences, tear off the roof and find restoration in the power of God's Word.

When religion crowds you out, not allowing room for your need, pressing you to the back of the bunch, tear off the roof and enter the sanctuary of the compassion of Jesus. The cross and forgiveness are for everyone. "Whosoever calleth on the name of the Lord shall be saved."

No Cynicism in Faith

In the story, the Pharisees were too busy inspecting the minister to expect a miracle. Their skepticism kept them from the blessings Jesus could bestow upon them. His healing was not just reserved for the derelicts and cripples, but was also for the educated, the clerically elite, and doctors of the law; yet they were so full of venom, they missed the Christ's virtue.

Even those who have reached the top, becoming well-known in their area of expertise, must lower themselves to be liberated. You can reach the pinnacle of success, but the lack of humility and honest self-evaluation will only bring eventual failure. Humility engenders heavenly help. The fact that the cripple's friends went up to let him down was moving to Jesus, inspiring the

Savior to reward their desperate faith in the face of the impossible.

Life truly is full of ups and downs. But in the case of these four friends and the lame man, the rollercoaster journey was the necessary route for restoration.

Don't let the cynicism of hypocritical witnesses, lying politicians or irreverent celebrities impede your sensitivity. Stay focused. Look up. Tear the roof off bitterness and betrayal.

Faith is believing God will respond to your impossible crisis. Cynicism is believing your impossible crisis is just another reason why God won't respond.

Faith climbs the mountain of impossible circumstances, knowing that you will eventually rise above fear, rejection, and rage. Cynicism is the pharisaical spirit that looks at the mountain and says, "That's absurd." There is no effort to try, only criticism of others who do try.

So I encourage you to defeat cynicism with renewed faith. Tear off the roof of timeworn indifference. Take that chance again. Don't just climb up on the roof of your dreams: *tear the roof off.* You may be surprised at God's miraculous response to the impossible.

Chapter Eight

Unveiling a Prince
(Judges 4)

The glimmering river of Kishon snaked through the Esdraelon plain, slithering between Mt. Gilboa and Mt. Tabor, and emptying into the Mediterranean Sea. The sun appeared as a golden eye set deeply in the gray clouds above. Sunflowers in the field leaned their yellow-rayed heads in the wind, bowing as if for solemn prayer, perhaps aware that drops of blood from battle would soon stain their delicate petals.

The dome-shaped summit of Mt. Tabor hid behind a misty curtain of white, with black garments of a tempest enfolding the heavens to the east. Rows of corn stretched upward on the narrowing slopes. Claps of thunder, seemingly applauding the change of seasons, provoked bold strokes of lightning. The scene was a collage of brown dirt, scarce green trees, tender shoots of grass, a few exploring sheep, farmers tapping their staffs, and earth-toned villages. Rain was coming. Revolution would follow. Rest would remain.

Children skipped along the threading paths among the hills, some stopping to accept a generous drink of goat's milk from local shepherds. They trampled through thorny burnets, shrubs, and wild almonds. In their innocence, they were not aware of change; like a season of winter losing its chill and spring flowers pushing through soils of freedom, they would have to witness it to understand it, to believe in it, to know what liberty in God meant.

Deborah, a prophetess in Israel, convinced Barak, the self-effacing captain of the Jewish army, to face Sisera in battle. Deborah was a woman of contrasts: of silk and iron, kind eyes and magisterial words. She walked as a lady, but keenly discerned her times like a warrior, unafraid to stand against the dictatorial edicts of the Canaanite king, Jabin. Her faith was like the rigid rocks near a sea, unrelenting, immovable against the tide.

Twenty years of oppression had passed. One thousand and forty Sabbath days passed without rest for the Israelites, watching the 900 chariots of Jabin rumble through their land, instilling fear in the inhabitants and resentment in young dreamers. But at this prophetic point, Deborah knew that God was with her, and through her would initiate a shift of dominion. Israel would become a theocracy again. The heathen idols, polished by the hands of evil priests, would no longer receive the honor due Jehovah.

Sisera was the celebrated general of the enslaving armies of Canaan. Barak gathered 10,000 brave warriors from Naphtali and Zebulun and set out to confront the enemy.

Barak displayed renewed courage because the Word of God had been spoken. He need not fear vultures on this day, for death would serve the carrion birds the flesh of his enemies. Faith is a galvanizing force that turns hesitant leaders into bold executors of God's plan. Barak knew he needed more than a vision; he needed God's voice. And he believed the oracle of that voice would be Deborah. Her presence inspired confidence in the men, and Barak knew if Deborah was in the camp, God would remain in the cause.

Godly leadership has always been an inspiration to young people. Today's youth desire strong anchors of truth. Men and women who are not politically motivated but who burn with a fire of sincerity; a burning that will not be quenched by petty issues or matters of personal opinion. A man or woman of God who prays diligently and daily is the fixed link in the chain of hope, and like Deborah, provides stability for others who are weaker in faith.

In my life, there have been men and women that stimulated an appetite in me for the deeper things of God. They are fair and caring individuals who lead by example, not mere rhetoric. They genuinely love people. They show real interest in the successes of others and not just the fruits of their own labor. They have the spirit of Deborah: sturdy in trustworthiness, sensitive to the voice of God, and stouthearted in the face of adversity.

When you have strong leadership, the willingness to die for a worthy cause is not just an overused cliché. Barak knew Deborah represented a true reflection of the heartbeat of God, and for her he would risk his life and the life of his men. May God continue to raise up men and women with the spiritual mettle and gracefulness to lead oncoming generations into the battle for righteousness, joy, and peace in the Holy Spirit.

The rains fell in heavy, dark sheets, tiny nails of silver driving into the parched ground. The Kishon River drank thirstily of the heavenly refreshment, swelling at its banks. Sisera's men moved with plodding steps, mud smacking at their sandals, water soaking their feet with a deathly chill. Horses got bogged down in the slippery traps, and their hooves kicked, slinging mud, splattering the faces of fallen men.

Suddenly, arrows flew through the air. Men howled animal screams of agony. They were trapped with nowhere to run and nowhere to hide. The swelling river pulled at the dead bodies, swirls of crimson gurgling in the depths. Mud and blood. Tears and sweat. Death whispers and fading moans.

The archers laid down their bows and picked up swords, dashing down the narrow, slippery, steep grade, the rain ticking against their brazen shields. They attacked the Canaanites with swift fury, sharp blades slashing into exposed body parts where enemy soldiers had dropped their shields. A frenzy of battle sounds rent the air: bodies thudding, slapping, sloshing in the swampy conditions; swords clashing, axes crunching into bone, scraping rock and shooting sparks; men screaming in agony, gurgling bubbles in the swirling water; grunts of struggle, laboring arms and legs in strained hand-to-hand combat. In the end, the surprise attack left Canaan's forces sorely depleted.

Sisera, stunned by the disastrous results of the ambush, jumped off his horse and fled. Retreat was usually not a part of his strategy, but strategies change. The faces of the dead haunted Sisera as he fled — the blue lips peeled back, the teeth jutted in hunger for life, and the eyes staring into the bleakness of eternal black. He suffered flashbacks of swords stuck in the soft, wet earth, daggers plunged into the hearts of his best men, and bloodstained shields rammed among the rocks. His mind churned anxiously with memories of headless soldiers leaned against dead horses, stiff arms reaching for the hand of God, grimacing mouths poised to drink the bitter cup of mortality. He rubbed his eyes, massaged his temples, and shook his head, trying to dispel the graphic images.

He could still smell the putrefying flesh, the nauseating stench of eviscerated bellies and urine, the coppery scent of blood, the miasmic soup prepared by the grim reaper. Shadows of the dead loomed over his shoulder, hallucinations of skinless men chasing him. At times, Sisera thought he saw the elongated blade of Death's sickle, the curve of finality ready to strike. He ran faster, his heart thudding harder and harder, threatening to burst from his rib cage. Wheezing, he labored to suck in air. The clouds had parted and the burning rays of the sun cooked him on his desert passage of escape, hinting at the fires of doom at the "dead" end of his life.

In the distance, Sisera saw a lone tent standing surreally against a backdrop of oak trees and dancing lilies. He wiped the sweat from his eyes with the sleeve of his bloodstained tunic, smearing crimson where the beads of sweat had been. He recognized that the tent belonged to his good friend Heber, the Kenite. He suddenly felt hopeful. Sisera looked over his shoulder, checking the sand and sage for any movement. He saw none. He moved forward, his tense muscles relaxing, feeling safer with each step toward the tent.

Jael, the wife of Habor, gazed out at the approaching warrior. She recognized his square, furrowed face, the bull neck and heavy shoulders, the gray, curly hair, peppered with blood and dust. He looked 10 years older than their last meeting a few weeks earlier.

She hurried to meet him. Her smile and congenial manner softened Sisera. He felt safe as she urged him to take cover in their tent. The smell of jasmine and her feminine kindness sedated him. He had been running with the fuel of fear, and suddenly he felt drained, spent of all fighting power. He lay down upon a bed made of furs and feathers while Jael covered him with a mantle.

"Please, give me some water, for I am very thirsty," he said.

She poured some milk from a leather bag. The soured milk is what the Arabs call *leban*. Drinking a large quantity of the refreshing drink made Sisera even more tired. He was worn out from fighting, running, worrying, and fearing a sudden strike by the hand of Barak. *Barak* means "lightning," and even when he closed his eyes, Sisera could see the rapid stroke of phosphorescent bolts, the quickened sword of Barak.

Jael, assured by Sisera's heavy breathing and piggish snores, calmly retrieved a tent peg in one hand, and clasped a mallet in the other. Moving with the precision of a butcher, she placed the peg on Sisera's temple, raised her arm, dropped the mallet, and drove the tent peg through his skull. He died instantly. Explosions of crimson brought speeding stars of doom. The spirit of Sisera surged to the Maker, his body lying cold and harmless in a frozen state of shock.

Barak arrived shortly after the execution. He

searched out the tent of Jael, only to find that his dirty work had already been done. The body lay limp on the tent canvass, its mantle an emblem of death, soaked with the blood of a fallen evil. The curtain of an empire's oppression of Israel was lifted, allowing freedom's light to shine again.

The beautiful thing about the events just described was that Deborah had already declared the outcome of the battle in Judges 4:9, "...the Lord shall sell Sisera into the hand of a woman."

Your Enemy Can't Get Ahead

The victory was stated before the battle started. Prophecy preceded the predator. If we stay in the light, walking in the projection of God's prophetic word, we will be able to see pitfalls before we fall into them. Discernment is predicated on our obedience to His Word. When we trust God's Word, howling wolves of darkness will never be able to trap us outside of God's help. Temptation will have no hold on our minds. Greed's hand will have no grasp on our intentions.

This doesn't mean that failure is forever avoided, but it does mean that our chances of sinful entrapment lessen in the light of truth. We need to keep the light on. Darkness cannot intimidate children who walk in the light.

> *Therefore judge nothing before the time, until the Lord come, who both will bring to light the hidden things of darkness, and will make manifest the counsels of the hearts: and then shall every man have praise of God* (1 Corinthians 4:5).

Our Enemy Can't Hide

We cannot hide from heaven. The enemy may think his clandestine schemes and movements are undetectable, but Sisera soon found out that God had Sisera "pegged" from the start. Sisera came looking for a hiding place, and ended up in a dying place.

Satan tries to sneak in the back door of our faith; he tries to hurt us through people we care deeply about. But when we stay in God's light, the instructions of His Word, we may still be wounded, but we don't have to be fooled. God will give us open eyes — discernment to know where the adversary will try to attack next. This doesn't mean we need to be suspicious of everything around us. If we simply stay in the Word, our love for God and consistent journey through the Scriptures will sharpen our spiritual senses to the deceptions of the devil.

Our Enlightenment Will Happen

The situations we face may seem impossible because of oppression and unfulfilled promises. But the story of Deborah teaches us not to rely on the control of the past, but on the considerations of God's purpose. Deborah prophesied that a woman would bring victory before the day was done. That prophecy carried more weight than 20 years of enslavement and taxation by Canaan.

What oppressions are keeping you from focusing on the promises God has made to you? Jesus Christ is the same yesterday, today, and forever. Maybe a Jael type of faith is standing by, just waiting to strike out at an old enemy that brings doubt or fear. God sees that area of oppression. He knows exactly where it is lodged. It may be in you now, but a little faith, mixed with a lot of prayer, will draw it out, and then victory will be yours. Your circumstances, and the dream of triumphing over past feelings and failures, are not impossible, they are impending — waiting for you to walk in the light and confidence of God's Word.

Chapter Nine

Boundaries of the Supernatural
(Genesis 15)

The restless patriarch stared up at the blinking stars. He traced various stars with imaginary lines, outlining the perfect symmetry of God's city. Pinnacles of ornate design seemed to visibly light up as he focused on his dream of a utopian land where God ruled and peace resided. The man yearned for the inevitable encounter, the ethereal discovery, but it seemed so far out of reach.

The sight of the imposing peaks of the mountains east of Hebron, rising over 2,600 feet, gave the man brief moments of peace. Abraham was on a quest orchestrated by God, one that transcended human boundaries — a journey of faith...a path of promise...a destination of divine origin.

God had promised to be a protective shield around Abraham, guarding against any dark forces that would attempt to destroy the covenant. There might be times of trouble ahead for Abraham's descendants, but this covenant would remain constant and transform future adversity into channels for divine purpose. Nations would rise up against the Jews, plots of genocide would seep from the bowels of hell, and Abraham's descendants would disperse, but despite every destructive attempt of Satan or man, this agreement would still stand.

The days moved slowly, like an old man stepping in tar pits. Abraham felt more anxious with each passing day. He often wondered if his majestic God was even at home. Abraham's dreams took on greater shape at night. He envisioned prodigious mountains in the background, pristine waters zigzagging down the verdant slopes, peaceful homes filled with heirs of promise, families gathered around luxuriant tables topped with abundant fruits and lavish meats. But, would it ever come true? Would this dream ever become a reality?

While fireflies danced through the air on a nearby hill, Abraham continued to stare, to wonder, to dream.

Oh, how often we dream it but fail to do it. As I look back on some of my own dreams, I realize that the reality of those dreams' fulfillment never quite lived up to my expectations. Winning a certain basketball game was not as exciting as I had envisioned — it didn't depend upon a last-second shot which, of course, I would make. Preaching a particular message didn't quite bring the hoped-for results. Counseling with a couple about their marriage didn't yield the pearls of wisdom I had envisioned before the meeting.

How about you? Have you ever felt that same wide chasm between your dream and reality? You just knew your boss wanted to meet with you to offer you a raise — until you got fired. You fixed your husband his favorite meal, thinking he would lavish you with praise — and then he brought home takeout. You were sure the alternative medicine recommended by the doctor would clear up the problem this time — only it got worse.

The clanging of pots in the distance brought Abraham back down to earth. The sound of grinding wheat and barley made his mouth water; he could already taste the sweetness of the bread. As he thought of food and drink — the satiating of his physical hunger — the voice of God interrupted with an unexpected Word that would feed his spiritual hunger for years to come:

"Do not be afraid, Abram. I am your shield, your very great reward."

Startled at first by the sudden visitation, Abraham looked in the direction of his Friend's voice and said, "O Sovereign Lord, what can you give me since I remain childless and the one who will inherit my estate is Eliezar of Damascus?"

God encouraged Abraham with the blueprints of His divine will, showing him that the seed of Abraham would be like the stars of heaven, innumerable light fixtures glowing in the homes of the celestial. God would build this from the loins of Abraham, but the foundation of this nation, Israel, would be forged through the darkness of slavery in Egypt. In the fourth generation, God would put the finishing touches on His masterpiece and draw the nation out of bondage into blessing.

There would certainly be heartaches and trials during the completion of the plan, but God would keep His Word. Persecution and promise would meld into something beyond human imagination, something never before seen in the history of dreams.

God instructed Abraham to prepare a sacrifice using

a heifer, a she goat, a ram, a turtledove, and a pigeon. Abraham quickly assembled the required animals, took hold of his knife, deftly sliced each ingredient of the immolation, and arranged them in parallel lines, creating a path of promise. Blood oozed from the animals; the ground was moistened red. Abraham prepared a highway of holiness, an avenue for the Almighty.

Birds of prey squawked on winds of death, spiraling toward the raw meat and bloodstained ground. Their hooked bills closed in fast, and Abraham could see the black, beady eyes of these carrion hunters. Symbolically, these vultures represented the future enemies of Israel — enemies that would seek to devour the offspring of Abraham. But as Abraham fought them off, sending them back to the skies, so God would raise guardians to protect the seed of Abraham from annihilation.

And so, throughout the ages, prophets have been sent to fight against hellish predators. Just as Abraham waved off the flesh-eating birds, present-day men of God wave off attacking demonic spirits that come to devour our sacrifices, our living service of praise and worship. Pastors must fight off rebellion that springs from modern temptations — spirits of lust and perversion that seek to consume youthful imaginations. Parents chase away atheistic ideologies planted in their children's minds by unrighteous teachers and remove the confusion of evolution from the truth of Creationism. There are scores of demonic buzzards circling the spiritual atmosphere of America, anxious to feed off vulnerable minds. They represent the baser instincts of our sinful nature. These spirits see our young people as their feeding ground. We must determine to fight them off and preserve our next generation of living sacrifices in the Kingdom of God.

Abraham's daydream faded into the darkness. He yawned, stretched, and entered his tent for the night. In a matter of minutes he drifted into deep slumber, his gentle snores wafting through the desert. And in his sleep, Abraham again dreamed. In his dream, a dark hole formed, a swirling pit of terror into which Abraham fell quickly. But then God spoke to him.

As the burning furnace of His Presence blazed through the rows of sacrificial meat, God outlined Abraham's future: "To your descendants I give this land, from the river of Egypt, the Euphrates, the land of the Kenites, Kenizzietes, Kadmonites, Hittites, Perizzites, Rephaites, Amorites, Canaanites, Girgashites and Jebusites."

The Boundaries of the Supernatural

Within the boundaries of the sacrificial walked sovereignty. God did not choose to move through the pieces of sacrifice until darkness came. A need for fire is recognized at night more than in the day. Darkness typifies suffering, and in the midst of suffering comes the fire of covenant. For Abraham, God passing between the severed animals was a sign of oneness, a fiery agreement with Abraham that neither time nor trouble could destroy.

God reserved His greatest glory for the extreme darkness. How fitting is that in relation to our suffering? The greatest display of God's presence and power in our lives comes when the sun has gone down on our ambitions, and the darkness of regret and fear has closed in.

His glory thrives in our blindness of purpose. When we cannot see what will develop with the plans we've laid out in perfect order, His revelation of grace steps on the scene, lights up the night with blazing love, passes through our pain, and leaves a path of promise to follow.

It is a path of flesh and fire, of harmony between our weaknesses and His divine strength. It is a trail of truth that will help us find our way to peace. The divided flesh of our dreams tells God that we are subject to the sword of His truth, and the burning lamp of His presence tells us that He will never leave us nor forsake us. Just as God passed as a smoking furnace between the halved animals of Abraham, the furnace of passion for His kingdom dwells in the midst of our heart, where sensual craving is divided from spiritual need.

If you are weary, living too distant from your destiny, step back within the boundaries of the supernatural. It may require that you sacrifice your plans for God's plans, but in the end, you will have the passion of God. You will forsake the swamplands of frustration for the borders of promise.

Boundaries are somewhat like arms, and the arms of God wait to enshroud you. You've had pain. You've endured heartache. Now, faith ignites as the heavenly Father embraces you, and you know your trail of suffering has been exchanged for a path of peace.

Chapter Ten

Dreamers

A dreamer doesn't always make sense. Sometimes he sounds like a child with a mouth full of jaw-breakers, for he speaks in seemingly unintelligible gibberish that one presumes will never amount to anything. And when the dreamer tries to articulate what he is envisioning, it is often viewed as crazy or impractical. But the dreamer just shrugs off the criticism and, rather than becoming discouraged, continues to hold fast to his dreams. In response, listeners might wag their heads, shrug their shoulders, laugh, grunt cynically, and then give him a lengthy lecture on reality.

But dreamers don't think in terms of reality. They're not oblivious to it — they just don't live within its boundaries. The imposed limitations of negative onlookers, cynical bystanders, and dubious critics drive the dreamer to private chambers of prayer, where in secret he communes with God.

God attaches a ladder to your dream when the world fences you in — just ask Jacob. God put a bare-legged, shieldless, swordless stone-thrower in a valley with a towering heathen champion who carried over 500 pounds of brass armor. Why? Because God is a dreamer, too. Just ask David — he was the stone-thrower.

Is It Too Good to Be True?

When the Lord turned again the captivity of Zion, we were like them that dream (Psalm 126:1).

What made it feel like a dream as the psalmist watched the pilgrimage of his people back to their ancestral grounds? What made it seem like a foggy glimpse of joy birthed from a night vision? The psalmist saw laughter, and the tongues that once moaned of loneliness in a strange land were singing. It had to be a dream because laughter had long been hidden in the pool of lamentation. How could there be singing when the skies of freedom had long been grayed by the clouds of Babylonian domination?

But the fact is, someone had dreamed of this moment. Someone, or some group of hope-reviving, never-say-die intercessors went to bed every night with one thought on their mind: returning to Jerusalem. And when their eyes closed at night, they drifted into dream-like regions where, painted on the screens of their imaginations, were the rolling hills of home. And God rewarded their dreams with moments of fulfillment, in which the dreamer would say, with tears in his eyes, "This is too good to be true!" God's response would be, "It's too true to be good — it's the best." As the psalmist joyfully wrote, "The Lord hath done great things."

God's blessings to us are not ordinary. They are not cheap, run-of-the-mill, temporary emotional frenzies with no eternal value. Instead, God's gifts to us are priceless: a mountain of gold, a river of diamonds, and a sea of silver. And even then, the price tag of His mercies is too excessive for earthly comparison. For we were not bought with gold and silver, but with the precious blood of the Lamb. His blood, our blessing; His sacrifice, our satisfaction; His pain, our pleasure. We should thank God every day for the moment we were allowed to exit the confines of our Babylon of sin and death.

The Israelites had known extreme sadness, not ecstasy. They had dwelt in the prisons of shame, not the palaces of prosperity. It had been a long time since they had drunk from the cup of merriment, for the bitter seeds of sorrow had been their wine. The Jews could never find happiness in the culture of Babylon. The call of Jerusalem was too strong. The longing in their collective soul to return to their homeland could never be appeased by the delicacies of Babylon.

It's Too God to Be Trite

II Corinthians 3:17 states, "Where the Spirit of the Lord is, there is liberty," but where the spite of the land is, there are only memories of freedom and mourning for one's homeland. One step beyond the gate of bondage lies the liberating air of joy — and the whole world takes on a different color. It no longer emits the gray pallor of sin and death, but it shines with rosy skies and blossoming fields of peace. When the bonds of failure fall behind us, we want to climb the highest mountain and sing loudly for everyone to hear — even if we can't sing!

Seldom do we find more than what we expected in our present world. Too often, we find less: less character in those entrusted with great power and less value in material things we paid too much for. We discover a politician is for sale; an athlete is leading a double life; a minister is dishonest. But God is full of surprises and derives great joy out of exceeding our human, finite expectations. We think we have God figured out as we carry around our little cups waiting for His rain. . . then CRASH! A flood pours out of the heavens. We should have been bringing barrels out on trolleys. We expected a cup; God filled a canyon. The seed of faith teaches us that although the seed is small in size, it is not small in expectation. The seed of faith knows that an orchard will break forth in due season.

Oh, how Zacchaeus must have felt when Jesus turned in his direction and announced that they would share lunch at his house! "Zacchaeus, come down immediately. I must stay at your house today" (Luke 19:5 NIV). As Zacchaeus inched down the sycamore, nervously looking around at the others, his heart beating furiously against his rib cage, he must have thought he was in a dream. Jesus didn't just give him a cordial nod from a distance (an acknowledgement that alone would have made Zacchaeus' day), He actually invited Himself over. Jesus doesn't simply acknowledge us; He comes to visit. And He doesn't just stay for a quick cup of coffee; He's planning on a full-course meal. Jesus certainly exceeded Zacchaeus' expectations. You see, Jesus became more than a dream — He became a dinner guest.

Imagine how the woman caught in adultery must have felt when God, the maker of the law, robed in flesh, the vehicle of grace, stepped in to save her from death. In her wildest dreams, she could never have imagined that the Savior would come to her rescue, pulling her from the stones of condemnation. She was caught in more ways than one. The Pharisees caught her in the act of adultery, but Jesus caught her in the arms of mercy.

If someone would have told her a day before that the most innocent man to ever live, the cleanest citizen to ever dwell on earth, the most powerful prophet to ever open His mouth, would step in front of the Sanhedrin and save her from death, she would have rolled her eyes, sighed in utter disbelief, and told that person that he had been eating too much leavened bread mixed with new wine.

For the destitute living behind thick walls of shame, it usually seems too far-fetched to believe in change. The sun would have to get stuck in space and cease to offer daylight before their lives could change. But, like Mary Magdalene and Zacchaeus, many have discovered that the Son did get stuck, on a path to a cross where three nails would hold Him for six hours, and the light of grace would forever shine on the disconsolate.

It's Too God to Be Trivial

I have a category of dreams I call "disposable dreams." These are the kind that last a few days and then get thrown onto the trash heap of impossibilities. You get a fleeting thought. You think you can conquer the world; but then you remember that you are not made of steel and titanium, merely flesh and bone. So you back away from fantasies of being a victor and settle for something more down-to-earth, something not quite so mountainous.

Maybe this happened when you were a child and thought you would be the next Babe Ruth. Then, after a season or two of zero home runs, you begin to think you are more like the candy bar than the player. You go into your inventory of dreams, snatch that one off a shelf, and toss it out the window onto the trash bin of "maybe I'd better try something else."

Dreams come in all sizes. And they vary in color, too. The most important dreams we mentally highlight in yellow, a shade we'd use to mark an important part of a book. Something we want to remember. But after a few disappointments, the highlight fades, and its place in the book of dreams is no longer earmarked.

The big dreams are the ones that will take many years to fulfill. They energize us with ambition. They feed our emotions. They dominate the screens in our sleeping visions. You study for this type of dream. You endure storms for it. You will reshape your life to get it, putting yourself through torturous transformations if need be to achieve your dream.

I'm God's, and I Won't Be Tormented

Ever had a bad dream you were absolutely delighted to wake up from? You are feeling the sweat on your forehead, the leftover dew from the nightmare. Yet, you are thankful to be back in the real world, wiping the droplets from your face. The hideous, fragmented memories of the nightmare melt away into your subconscious. You rise to eat breakfast: scrambled eggs, a couple of crisp, brown pieces of toast covered with your favorite jelly, a steaming cup of espresso. And you step back into the morning routine you are now extremely grateful for.

Recently, a close relative of mine told me about a disturbing dream he had. In the dream, contrary to the type of man he was, he shot someone. Although it was in self-defense, the police came and shuttled him off to iron bars and vicious-looking inmates. He would spend the rest of his life in prison. This man told me that, in the dream, he kept repeating to himself, "I hope this is a dream. This is not me. I would never do something like this!"

What about tortured minds that can't wake up? Because the dream they are in — the nightmare full of broken memories and repressed violence — is not a sub-conscious projection. It's real life. And it's really the worst.

It's a stark reality of trembling hands and reddened eyes scratched by the fingernails of terror. The lone figure of horror, dressed as a killer in black, flowing robes, is not some imagined evil from a book. It is reality for some people. It lives with them. Perhaps you have been in its prison, shackled to the cold, brick walls of shame. How do you wake up from this nightmare?

You are all sons of the light and sons of the day. We do not belong to the night nor to the darkness (I Thessalonians 5:5).

To the injured men or women trying to forget these nightmares, live free from the clawing memories that lacerate their emotions, and distance themselves from the self-pity that springs from distrust, they need to re-alize that they belong to someone else.

We belong to a compassionate, heavenly Father who wants to embrace us, caress our tear-stained cheeks with His tender hands, and lovingly gaze into the depths of our pain with His understanding eyes. We belong to

Jesus. The nightmares of abuse, self-inflicted wounds, and mutilating memories of past relationships no longer need to be our mental address. We *can* think differently.

So the next time the hooded knight of shame gallops into your life, lancing your soul with condemnation and guilt, stand up with a new shield of light and say, "I don't belong to you anymore. Since I met Jesus and was born again, I have found a new home, a new way of thinking about myself. I am not the ugly things the nightmares of life have said I am. I am a child of God. I exist for Him and Him alone."

Chapter Eleven

Called to a Higher Purpose

People around the world are disappointed with life. Many are disgruntled with their education or feeling they should have chosen a different field. Others are dissatisfied with their experiences, wishing something more adventurous would happen to them.

People of the 21st century are not easily enamored with life. Sunsets and softball wane in the eyes of the discontented. Restless baby boomers want bigger homes and better incomes. Postmodern minds require extreme feats of athleticism, stunts, or reality twists. It seems, in our fast-paced society, that few are satisfied with simplicity.

As I am writing, I pause to read a newspaper article concerning an illusionist, Criss Angel. To bring thrills to himself and a crowd of onlookers, he spent 24 hours in a 220-gallon water tank. It was a phone booth-sized contraption made of clear plastic and steel. He emerged the next day with crinkled skin, bloodshot eyes, and a dangerously low body temperature. He screamed a celebratory cry just before vomiting and passing out. All in the name of entertainment and adventure.

Not everyone goes to these extremes to break from

tradition. And while some attempts to be daring and unconventional are merely masochistic, there is something to be said for a sincere seeker of God who throws caution to the wind. We don't have to sink into a 220-gallon tank of water to prove our mettle, but we should sink to our knees a little more often, in search of the grander moves of God.

In John 2, Jesus and His disciples attended a wedding in Cana of Galilee. Cana was located in the land west of the Sea of Galilee, about six miles northeast of Nazareth. It was called "Cana of Galilee" to distinguish it from another Cana, inhabited by the tribe of Ephraim. The route from Nazareth to Cana was cloaked with marshy stretches and reeds, for the name "Cana" means "place of reeds."

Imagine the disciples following the steady steps of Jesus along the soft, wet trail to Cana. Occasionally, they plucked pomegranates from nearby trees, playfully breaking the rough, reddish rind to suck out the delicious, juicy seeds. Some of the disciples were not as skilled at eating the messy fruit and left deep red stains, like drops of blood, on their robes. Walled in by countless Valonica oak trees, nature's merciful canopy of interlacing branches shielded them from the fierce heat of the sun. They enjoyed a cool, refreshing breeze which carried the scent of mountain lilies — a fitting ambiance for a wedding. In the days ahead, much disarray, heartache, and loneliness would assault the spirits of the disciples, but for now there was only peace.

Soon they arrived at the wedding, shook the dust off

their sandals, washed their feet, exchanged pleasantries with the hosts, and took their places at the feast. Music abounded. Laughter and dancing filled the air with a sense of timeless merriment, lifting the hearts of the guests above their worries over Roman domination. Everyone's lips glistened with wine. Rose bouquets shivered in cool breezes. The pageantry surrounding the bride and groom brought a measure of hope and vision for the future. The dry, crusted grounds of barren dreams were buried beneath the celebration of matrimony. Maybe this was one of the reasons Jesus decided to attend a wedding so early in His ministry: to give a hint of the joys of the future Kingdom of heaven, once His sacrifice was married to the atonement for sins.

At some point during the feast, Mary, the mother of Jesus, approached her Son with an urgent request. Mary was a woman of great presence. She walked with gracefulness and, even though she wore the raiment of a peasant, she exuded the elegance of a wealthy queen. Though time had etched a few wrinkles on her face, she still glowed with benevolent radiance.

Mary gazed affectionately at Jesus.

"They have no wine," she said, nodding toward wedding party, a little anxious.

Jesus turned to her and, mildly reproving, replied, "Woman, what have I to do with you, my hour is not yet come." By this He meant that the first supply of wine was not entirely exhausted yet, and until then, He would not be solicitous.

Mary's sense of servitude and compassionate nature must have overridden the slight correction she received from her Son, because she then turned and said to the servants, "Do whatever He tells you."

Jesus smiled at His mother and glanced over at His disciples to see if they were watching. Then He turned and focused on some stone water pots.

Water pots were ritual staples for cleansing in the Jewish culture. As guests would enter the home or exit after a meal, they would rinse their hands in these pots. These particular water pots mentioned in John 2 could hold 20 gallons of water each. On this day, Jesus decided to use them for a higher purpose.

He pointed to the pots and told the servants to fill them to the brim with water. Apparently, the water pots were sitting empty. The six pots had capacity, but no content. So Jesus recognized 120 gallons of potential.

There is a parallel between the human mind and the water pots of stone. The water pots were appointed for a menial task of cleaning the dirt off someone's hands. In other words, a water pot was simply a place in which to deposit filth. A human mind given to the ways of the world is not much different. It can also be a place to deposit filth, collect perverted tendencies, or store unrighteous fantasies. A person whose life has been a repetitious ride of heartbreak and failure may feel that they are merely containers for accumulating miseries. No peace in sight. No happiness in the home. No joy in the insipid job. No recovery from past abuse or present maltreatment.

After the servants filled the pots with water, Jesus instructed them to give a taste of this water to the governor of the feast, the man responsible for the entertainment, food, and format of the wedding. And when the governor of the feast tasted the miracle formula, his eyebrows shot up in amazement.

Up to this point, the servants had been inconspicuous. They wore drab, earth-toned tunics and didn't put on elaborate airs. They were dutiful and mindful of every detail requested by the host. But, ironically, it was the servants alone who were in on a secret that, usually, only the master of the house would know. They knew that this new wine came from the supernatural, not the supermarket. They had poured the water into the enormous containers only moments before, likely sneaking a sip to refresh their dry, thirsty mouths. They all knew a transformation had occurred.

The governor, still brimming with excitement about the discovery, called for the bridegroom. He commended him for bringing the best wine out last, which was quite unusual in most circumstances. While lavishing praises upon the bridegroom, it never occurred to the ruler that Jesus was actually responsible for the new supply of wine. But the servants knew.

———•••———

In this amazing miracle, I find myself. Like the water pots used for something greater than hand washing, I am called to a higher purpose. I am not made for the deposit of filth, but for the indwelling of God's spiritual fire. I am not a container of condemnation, or a vessel merely reserved for the baser acts of vice, or a receptacle of earthly rejection and fears. I am a child of God, and I hold in my earthen vessel a treasure of truth

> *But we have this treasure in earthen vessels, that the excellency of the power may be of God, and not of us* (II Corinthians 4:7).

The mind of the Christian is not a place for the defiling hands of sin indulgers to deposit ungodly concepts. The Christian mind is called to a higher purpose — to be transformed from ordinary thoughts to extraordinary revelations. As a Christian, I am admonished to have the mind of Christ.

We all know that bad habits can be hard to break. The barriers of mediocrity stand tall for the man who lacks righteous ambition. Mountains of ministries await the eager efforts of men and women who dare to challenge the unknown. But one can't climb to new heights without leaving behind the base camp formalities — those establishments that often mark the decline of progress. The formalities I'm speaking of are not the doctrinal or moral kind, but rather the restrictions on faith that are imposed by people who are smug and satisfied in their "religion." These are the ones who have no desire to grow anymore or to share their testimony beyond the few in their small circle of influence.

But there are others who cannot be satisfied with their past performances. They want to continue upward in the quest to be more like Jesus. They want God to transform their lives into fountains of hope that quench the thirst of society.

You see, in John 2, Jesus took ordinary vessels and revealed an extraordinary transformation — changing the liquid from water into wine. He could have chosen new leather wineskins from the marketplace in which to put the new wine. But He chose water pots of stone, vessels carved out of the nearby rocky hills, normally created for only one purpose.

Within the body of Christ are a great number of

people who don't feel worthy to be used. They feel inferior to others because of past mistakes, bad memories, and personal inadequacies. But the plain stone water pots in this story stand as monuments of hope for the struggling Christian. You don't have to be beautiful or perfect or possess a long list of capabilities and achievements. God does not always choose what's pretty, but He will hear who's prayerful. In this day of stress, depression, and even terrorism, God still wants to use ordinary people, like the water pots of stone, who are carved out of the hard places of life.

Chapter Twelve

Down for the Count

*After the Philistines had captured the ark of God,
they took it from Ebenezer to Ashdod. Then they carried the ark into Dagon's temple and set it beside
Dagon. When the people of Ashdod rose early the next
day, there was Dagon, fallen on his face on the
ground before the ark of the LORD! They took Dagon
and put him back in his place. But the following
morning when they rose, there was Dagon, fallen on
his face on the ground before the ark of the LORD!
His head and hands had been broken off and were
lying on the threshold; only his body remained. That
is why to this day neither the priests of Dagon nor
any others who enter Dagon's temple at Ashdod step
on the threshold (1 Samuel 5:1-5 NIV).*

The Philistine city of Ashdod was electrified as soldiers brought in the Ark of the Covenant. Cheering
crowds were mesmerized by the sheer beauty of the
golden ark, ignoring its significance to the Jews. Ashdod
was situated between Ashkelon, a seaport, and Ekron,
inland on the caravan route going east to Lydda and
west to Joppa. It was one of the five principle cities of

the Philistine empire, and its location certainly en-
hanced its military and economic status.

The inhabitants of Ashdod gave their allegiance to
one major deity in their pantheistic universe: Dagon.
Dagon was the fish god, a god of agriculture and fertility.
It was half-man and half-fish — a male mermaid. The
head and hands had human features, and the body was
that of a fish.

The Ark of the Covenant, confiscated from a de-
feated Israel, was placed in the temple of Dagon. The
people patronized the earthly throne of Jehovah, setting
it before Dagon as an inferior subject.

The priests of Philistia, stoic and methodical, full of
pride over their pagan deities, treated the ark with dis-
dain. They didn't care if smudges from fingerprints were
left or layers of dust from the journey settled on the
prized spoil. The blessing of Israel at the moment was no
more than the bounty of Philistia. Hatred brewed in the
priests' eyes. Their fastidious preparations were impres-
sive to watch, but truly worthless in the presence of the
momentarily quiet Jehovah. But, He would soon speak.

While the priests went about their nighttime activities, dancing feverishly beneath the sparkling stars,
staring superstitiously at the silvery disk of the full
moon, things at the temple of Dagon seemed safe and secure. But the heathen statue could not stand before
God's statute. Hell's reflection gave way to the source of
true light. The shadow of deception, the fraudulent
figure of fertility, toppled before the absolute power of
creation. No matter how grand the temple, with ornate
pillars and fluted columns, manicured greenery and
arched entrances, it was no longer a sanctuary or safe
haven for the lifeless Dagon.

A wind of glory, a gust of divine disgust, whipped against the colossal relic, accompanied by a creaking sound and a rusty screech. At first the statue leaned to one side, as if straining to hear a mortal's plea for mercy or groveling request. Then, crash! It fell to the ground.

The priests scurried about, propping the idol back in place. They brushed away dust and polished every inch of the male mermaid, swimming in affection, drowning in seduced adulation. They bowed and kissed the lifeless god in the shadow of the Creator, only a few feet away from the one true God.

Soon they returned to their routines, confident that Dagon would not stumble again. They prepared their sacrifices, ate festively and belched out empty words of wisdom concerning Dagon.

Meanwhile, Dagon stood erect before the throne of God, a miniature challenge for the One who spoke blazing suns and traveling stars into existence. This was like putting a clumsy amateur in the boxing ring with Muhammed Ali in his prime. Dagon didn't have a chance. One more swift, majestic breath of wind, and the knockout punch was delivered. Dagon teetered like a drunken man, wobbling back and forth on the pedestal, headed for his final destination: the canvas of defeat.

The sounds of destruction again shattered the quiet: the creak of the statue's leaning, the boom of stone and plaster hitting the ground, and finally, the snapping off of the statue's broken hands and head. This time, Dagon didn't survive the fall.

The priests were dismayed when they discovered the decapitated, handless Dagon. The priests' faces turned white, as if brushed by the stroke of death. Their eyes widened in horrific disbelief, mouths gaping open. Like maddened ants doused with gasoline, they scurried about frantically trying to salvage their deity. Tripping over one another and shaking their fists at each other, they argued loudly about what had happened. No doubt, some innocent bystander shouldered the blame for the incident and was possibly taken to be executed immediately.

A thin mist of white powder, the fine particles of the statue's caste, hung in the air. Unseen by the eyes of the priests were the angels clandestinely circling the temple, in the service of their Creator. Dagon couldn't upright himself. He was simply a form with no fountain of life. So when God knocked him down, there was no possible way he could get up. He was down for the count.

When, in the boxing world, is a fight declared a knock out? After the ten count. Dagon fell before the ark that contained the law of Moses. How many commandments were in the ark? Ten. Perhaps that is the reason why Dagon couldn't get up — because he was knocked down, spiritually, by the Word of God! The lifeless Dagon was no match for the living lawgiver.

Instead of "Down goes Frazier; down goes Frazier," I can imagine hearing that same taunt from angelic hosts, "Down goes Dagon; down goes Dagon!"

Don't Lose Your Mind

When the fear-stricken priests discovered that Dagon had fallen again, they feared his response; but, of course, Dagon could do nothing because he was stumped. It is good to stay on your face in prayer until God makes you whole, and you are able to return to your life clear-headed.

The disorienting elements of terrorism, economic instability, and family troubles can cause us, like Dagon, to lose our head. To calm those emotions, to stabilize our reactions, we all need those moments where we are on our knees, with our faces to the ground in deep intercession before God. Unlike Dagon, God will fix our head — our perspectives of life — and help us to rightly understand our past mistakes.

Have you been there, bewildered by broken promises and hasty decisions you've mistakenly made? In these moments, we need to ask God to raise us up after we have been knocked down — and sometimes knocked out — by the circumstances of life.

Let this mind be in you which was also in Christ Jesus (Philip. 2:5).

The first word in this verse is the key to the combination: "let." We often have to bring ourselves to a place where we allow the principles of Christ to work in us. Allow the anointing to break yokes of mental bondage. Allow the thoughts of love the opportunity to erase bitter memories. Allow the joy of the Lord to take over your thinking, where dark thoughts once lodged.

The other key word in the Scripture is "be." This word implies not only a dwelling, but a doing. There is an active element to this exhortation that must take place in our mind, otherwise, God's Word will become atrophied. In order for the Word of God to be effective in our lives, it must be exercised. It takes discipline to avoid the pitfalls of pessimism.

Don't Legitimize Your Mistakes

Restoration is only possible if God is involved in the process. We can revive a belief system, but if God is not intimately involved in the restoring of a heart and mind, then it becomes nothing more than a dry recitation, a one-way conversation with ourselves. We can refashion old lies, but in the end, they will lay worthless at the feet of the living God.

We shouldn't legitimize our mistakes by putting ourselves back in a place where we'll repeat them. The priests of Dagon tried to restore him back to his original state, but the original state was the problem. Dagon was not a god. He possessed no power, and only stood as a silent witness condemning the Philistines for their idolatry.

Failures yesterday can be learned from and transformed into future power, but if nothing is learned from them, then they just underscore a person's pride and stubborn will. We should not create a Dagon from our disappointments, repeating the same mistakes that go against God's plan for our lives.

If we are to be restored, let our souls be restored with the goodness of God. Let our hearts be restored with virtue and peace, and our minds with pure thoughts that transcend the New Age psychobabble of the day. Let our bodies be restored with reverent service and self-control, so that we are free to worship God without shame.

The pagan worshippers tried to restore Dagon to his previous state without recognizing that Dagon's fall was a sign that there was greater glory in God. Although we might not be as hedonistic as the Philistines, how often do we try to revisit what we have already learned doesn't work in the first place?

Don't Lose Your Meaning

The Philistines repositioned Dagon after he fell the first time. The second time he fell, his hands and head were severed.

A body without a head and hands is a body that has no authority and no capacity to work. In the end, Dagon was a lifeless fish unable to swim in the same divine depths as the Almighty. So truly, with regard to keeping company with Jehovah, Dagon was a fish out of water. In short, the work of dismantling an inferior relic of religious ignorance was, for God, just another easy effort.

As ineffective as the inanimate, lifeless caste of clay was, so are we when we dare to stand arrogantly before the holy God. We may boast of our successes, our inventions and our knowledge, but in comparison to our omniscient God, we are an empty, lifeless relic.

We may be sophisticated creatures, well-educated and good-mannered, but without the grace of God, our lives have little meaning. Our purpose in life is found solely through our relationship with our heavenly Father. To the Philistines, Dagon represented an escape from true reality. He was a substitute, a form of virtual reality, one fashioned by the hands of men, a contradiction to creation. Let us not fall into the trap of virtual religion without sweet communion with our King, thus regretting a spiritual day gone by — empty moments with no true substance.

Chapter Thirteen

Escape

Watch ye therefore, and pray always, that ye may be accounted worthy to **escape** *all these things that shall come to pass, and to stand before the Son of man* (Luke 21:36 emphasis mine).

In the middle of San Francisco Bay it sits, defiant against the sloshing, white-capped waves. The sun glares through massive beams of the Golden Gate Bridge upon the unsettling sight of isolation. Alcatraz is a concrete and steel memory sitting atop windswept sandstone. It was a fortress; it was a prison. It is now merely a tourist attraction from the past.

Within its haunting walls are 336 claustrophobic, windowless cells, measuring five by nine feet. The furnishings in each cell are spare: a narrow cot, a toilet bowl without a seat, a sink basin with only cold water, and two shelves and two thick boards fastened to a wall, one below the other, which serve as a table and chair.

The prison air is damp, as unseen devils play within its eerie shadows, and mice scurry where men once lived. Dank odors of brackish water and moldy walls assault the senses. There is a crushing sense of gloom within these walls, an aching emptiness, and whispers of sorrowful cries from the ghosts of chained men. You can almost hear the clanging of the double-locked doors shutting you in, imprisoning you away from love, peace and rest.

At times, in the early morning a pea soup fog hugs the bay, embellishing Alcatraz as a hellish structure arisen from an abyss of nightmares. It has quite the history of fear, a grim reminder of a place once inhabited by hardened criminals. You can imagine wraithlike figures roaming among the misty cloaked rocks, searching for an exit, waiting for a portal to open and a lonely sentence to end.

Helicopter blades pulsate above the San Francisco skyline. Horn-blowing yachts pass by. Large colonies of cormorants nest on the cliffs, western gulls make their home on the flattened top of the island, and black-crowned night herons dwell in the wildly dense vegetation. Some of the night herons have used their instinctive creativity to make a home, substituting twisted metal and cement for tree limbs. Tour boats taxi almost 500 people to and from the island during the daylight hours. It is a place to visit, an intriguing arena full of history.

Alcatraz was originally designed to keep the enemy out, then it was transformed to keep the enemy in. That is the difference between a fort and a prison. If you live in a fortress of faith, you keep unbelief out; but if you live in a prison of pride, you keep yourself chained to the doubts and fears within.

Alcatraz began as a place to store weapons and soldiers, but gradually it degraded to housing the wicked for life. Are you a harbor for hatred? Have you become a citadel of cynicism, holding criminal lusts and perverted affections in your heart, never letting them go, never setting them free? Are you shackled by shame? Chained by chastising memories? Haunted by trust-betraying hurt?

Breaking the Chains of Bitterness

There is a place in the heart where bitterness can get trapped. A place where there is no retreat from regret, no fleeing from failure, and no escape from scarring emotions. This place is unforgiveness.

A heart that harbors unforgiveness becomes somewhat like Alcatraz: a fortress in intent, but a prison in reality. The human heart was designed to house peace, sobriety, joy, and kindness; but anger, bitterness and envy become unwelcome residents for the children of God who dwell on betrayal and past mistakes.

No doubt, forgiveness is an escape from bitterness. When you can rejoice in the blessings of someone who has hurt you, then you know you have truly escaped the impossibility zone of bitterness. Bitterness binds while forgiveness frees. Choose forgiveness — it is the energy of compassion.

Breaking the Chains of Self

There hath no temptation taken you but such as is common to man: but God is faithful, who will not suffer you to be tempted above that ye are able; but will with the temptation also make a way to escape [emphasis mine], that ye may be able to bear it.

Wherefore, my dearly beloved, flee from idolatry (1 Corinthians 10:13-14).

"Idolatry" here means "image worship." We must flee the worship of self-image. Some people care more about how they look than who they love. Don't get locked down in narcissism, seeing only the good in yourself and the bad in others.

The word "escape" literally means "to exit." God helps the humble find a way out. He illuminates the exit signs that would otherwise be invisible to defiance and arrogance.

Acts of kindness are chain breakers. When we take our eyes off ourselves and begin to value the needs of others, we break the chain of selfishness. In this generation of prima donnas who demand payment to do anything, and of politicians who support both sides of an issue for the sake of money, it is refreshing to still hear people say "Yes!" to God, with no strings attached or hidden agendas.

Breaking the Chains of Isolation

*How shall we **escape**, if we neglect so great salvation; which at the first began to be spoken by the Lord, and was confirmed unto us by them that heard him* (Hebrews 2:3 emphasis mine).

Sometimes the threat of imprisonment doesn't come from outside attacks, but from inside neglect. You feel like running into a titanium house with no windows, locking the doors, and guarding the sensitive areas of your life.

During its run as a prison, Alcatraz was believed to be impossible to escape from. The choppy water surrounding the rocky island is a chilly 12 degrees Celsius (50 degrees Fahrenheit) year-round. Its churning depths offer only death; its sucking current invite only the brave. For anyone who tried to enter its waters, hypothermia would probably set in and immobilize him before he reached the shores of safety. You can imagine the muscles tightening, the uncontrollable shivering, and the loss of coordination when the swimmer can no longer control his limbs. The blood circulation slows, and the heartbeat weakens. Soon, the body becomes deadweight, sinking into the darkened abyss below.

As seconds, minutes, hours and days tick by for the prisoners, the island of isolation becomes more impossible to escape. The waters of sarcasm stay frigid. The depths of insecurity have much too strong a current to attempt escape. At some point, you even begin to lose the desire to be free, the sentence of shame and solitude becoming more familiar and, strangely, more sentimental.

You need to make a decision today to stop neglecting your soul. Instead, select a route of peace through the Word of God that will lead you off the island of self-pity. Select a starting point in prayer where you lay aside fear and begin to repair fragmented relationships. You see, when you neglect the needs of your spirit, you become somewhat robotic, eliminating the power of choice. In essence, you're saying you don't want to make a choice; you just want to hide.

So rise up in faith. Push away the prison bars of past betrayal that transported you to this Alcatraz state of mind. Don't ignore the fresh love God is bringing your way. Instead of running away from your problem, run toward God's promises, for they will bring you peace. Then peace brings spiritual contentment. Contentment ends containment. You won't feel like you need to be confined any longer, for you will be comfortable with the work God is doing in your life.

> *And now for a little space grace hath been shewed from the LORD our God, to leave us a remnant to* **escape**, *and to give us a nail in his holy place, that our God may lighten our eyes, and give us a little reviving in our bondage* (Ezra 9:8 emphasis mine).

The Wings of a Dove

How often does the broken heart plead for wings of escape? I imagine the hardened criminals at Alcatraz gazed longingly through their heavily barred windows, wishing to be the unchained birds of the island, free to come and go as they please, free to stretch their wings and catch a gust of wind that would sweep them high into the air.

How many of us are barred from blessings, imprisoned by pride, unable to soar in the Spirit because of self-imposed sentences of guilt and shame? Locked up in loneliness, unable to enjoy the freedoms of truth because we are haunted by yesterday's failures and tomorrow's uncertainty?

Robert Gilford, an ex-convict who spent over 37 years in Alcatraz, said of the D-block cell, "I'd walk around in circles until I collapsed, so I could sleep. Man, it was cold. I'd dream about food and dream I ate so much, I'd wake up with indigestion" (John Windrow, "A Walk to the Rock: From Chinatown to Alcatraz with an Insider's View," *Minneapolis Star-Tribune*, 19 February 1995, p 1).

There is a passage in Psalm 55 which is a cry of desperation from David. He is afraid of the terrors of death, the voice of his enemy, and oppression by the wicked. In the midst of entrapment he pens this poetic allusion, "Oh that I had wings like a dove! for then would I fly away, and be at rest" (v. 6).

So how does one escape from the painful prisons of the past? David gave us a clue when he talked about the "wings of a dove." The dove symbolizes the Spirit of God. The dove, a beautiful, white emblem of peace, is what we see settling upon the Messiah in the Jordan River at the beginning of His ministry.

After the death, burial, and resurrection of Christ, a new dimension of His Spirit was experienced on the day of Pentecost. What David could only dream of, sing about, and hope for became a reality in the gift of the Holy Spirit. In this way, we do have the wings of a dove to escape negative influences, painful memories and repressive spirits.

The way to escape the spiritual Alcatrazes of our lives is by getting in the Spirit. Romans 8:1 states,

There is therefore now no condemnation to them which are in Christ Jesus, who walk not after the flesh, but after the Spirit.

Maybe you've pursued lusts that have led to withered

hopes and dreams, but if you pursue God, He will lead you to the Rose of Sharon, the Lily of the Valley, to liberty. This means our pursuit of righteous attitudes and benevolent actions keeps us from the prisons of guilt and shame.

Jude tells us, "Pray in the Holy Ghost, building up your most holy faith." When we pray in the Spirit, it is like flying with the wings of a dove, escaping the traps of transgression, the cages of compromise, and the haunting holds of self- or man-inflicted hurt. We interject the presence of God, with His aura of peace and patience, when we seek Him fervently. We are able to take the wings of a dove, the spiritual mindset of God, and take flight from the environs of harm. This does not mean we become so heavenly-minded that we are no earthly good; rather, it's a matter of putting things in the right perspective.

The dove David mentioned in Psalm 55 is a turtledove. It is said, "Confined in a cage, they droop, and, like Cowper, sigh for `A lodge in some vast wilderness — some boundless contiguity of shade;' and no sooner are they set at liberty, than they flee to their mountains" (Dr. Thomson, *Land and the Book,* vol. 1, p. 416).

So, I have learned that when the trial is hot and the furnace of circumstances seems inescapable, to seek my Savior in prayer. And when His Spirit comes, I am set free to return to the purposes of His Kingdom. I realize that I am not designed for a cage, but for a cause. I do not have to be snared in a prison of ego and vindictiveness, but I can soar with love and peace in all things. I can escape by taking the wings of a dove!

Chapter Fourteen

Just Stepping Out for a Minute
(Matthew 14)

He wanted to step out. He wasn't sure what would happen. His heart felt like a crazed drum in his chest, and the pounding of the sea matched its rhythm. He lifted one leg over the wooden rail, careful not to rub against its sandpapery texture. He didn't want this adventure to begin with the embarrassment of a splinter stuck in his leg.

The air reverberated with noises that sounded like a battle was raging. Thunder cannoned, firing shots of fear into his heart. Lightning raced across the blackened sky, pressing its radiant fingers, jagged and arthritic, upon the sea. The rolling sea seemed much too dangerous to touch. It was an electric current of immeasurable power. *Maybe I should wait,* he thought. *Come back some other time to the realm of the supernatural. After all, I'm just a fisherman.* But in the distance, he saw the smiling face of his friend, his Savior, his God.

I can imagine him turning to his comrades, their faces stunned, their mouths gaping with astonishment. He looked back at the twisting sea. His foot touched the waves. He wasn't sure if he was shaking because the water was cold or because his nerves were. But, resolutely, he lifted his other leg over the railing.

He was so transfixed by what was happening that it took him a moment to realize that he was, indeed, standing on water. And not the frozen kind, either.

The briny depths seemed to whisper his name. His heartbeat accelerated to a pace he never thought possible, and he felt that, at any moment, his chest might explode, propelling his sprinting heart into the air, toward the angels.

He was no longer in his comfort zone. The waves rolled around him playfully, but he realized that this could be dangerous, like playing with a lion who might sink its teeth into you at any moment. He tried to keep his eyes on the calm, poised figure of Jesus, but the flashes and growls of the wind distracted him. His peripheral vision blinded his forward sight.

How often do we let this happen? The things to the left and right of our intended focus become the main target of concentration, until what we are supposed to be concentrating on is not even in view. Don't let the peripheral doubters distract you. Don't let misjudgments of the past keep you from concentrating on your miracle, your mission. Don't let the circumference of self-consciousness delay your progress as you seek to move forward toward the form of Christ you desire to be.

You tell your mind that your heart is just stepping out for a moment, going to go shopping for your dream. You've decided not to stay cooped up in fear, fatigued by other failures. You dress your heart in the finest hopes you can dig out of the closet. You reach for the doorknob of destiny. . .and then your mind speaks.

"Where are you going?"

"I'm just stepping out for a minute," you say.

"Is that right? Don't you remember what happened last time? You got lost!"

God Knows Your Heart

Could it be that a lost heart is often a runaway heart? Passion grows weary of waiting on rational observation. So the heart takes off into the unknown.

> *For if our heart condemns us, God is greater than our heart, and knoweth all things. Beloved, if our heart condemn us not, then have we confidence toward God* (I John 3:20-21).

Remember: God knows our heart. We may say things a certain way or act in accordance with the desires of another. But in our core being, in our truest self, that is the place where we know how we really feel. And God is there. He knows we want to step out, be different, and go places in the Spirit we've never been before.

We can trust God's translation of our heart. When we are confused about what we want, or about what we should do next, we can find out what God thinks about it. His Word is the unbroken compass to lead our heart out of thickets of fear and anger.

We may be tangled in other people's perception of us, unable to move forward in faith because we are stranded in needing to please them. All the while, our spiritual hearts weaken, and before long, we are hooked up to a life-support machine created by everyone else's approval.

But like Peter, an invitation from God has come. We feel drawn to do something beyond ourselves, beyond the need to impress others; we are simply driven by a need to be in God's presence, to do His Will. So we step out.

———•—•———

Meanwhile, Peter took his first step, an infant's explorations of the world of the miraculous. Jesus beamed like a proud father on the other end of the water route. Peter's steps were not the steps of a confident veteran of supernatural exercises. They were uncertain and hesitant for he was still a little scared. His teeth were chattering — whether from cold or anxiety was anyone's guess.

What next? The first step had to be the best. At least that's the way of the world. It doesn't get any better than the first taste. Ask the drug addict or the alcoholic. If we are not careful, we can slip into a state of boredom, once that thrill has waned. And, on a spiritual level, that can distract us from reaching more exhilarating stages of intimacy and faith.

Maybe that is why Peter began to sink. Maybe he wasn't just distracted by the storm. Perhaps he was distracted by the knawing feeling that, after that first step, everything would become routine and insidiously religious.

Peter was no longer balanced above the waves. He felt the trapdoor of reality open, and he began to sink. A look of terror replaced the smile of joy he'd had only moments before. The murky depths that had whispered his name earlier now grew louder. *If only the noise would go away!* he might have pleaded.

Why can't we eliminate the static of earthly temptations and distractions? It would be so much easier to hear the voice of God and act on what we've heard if the background noise would just fade away. But the fact is, we have to gain knowledge in the midst of noise. We have to trust what we've heard God speak to us in His Word before the storm showed up.

God Knots the Hope

Peter found out that God doesn't always create an elementary pathway for His disciples. If you are going to walk on water, it will not be on a cloudless day when the temperature is perfect, the sun is at its meridian, and the sea looks more like a platform of thick glass. The miracle is usually accompanied by storms such as demonic accusations, relationship challenges, criticism from others, physical illness, or our own lack of self-confidence.

God knots the hope. The knot is made of two laces: impossible odds, and His grace. We may think we can't overcome what we are facing right now, but Jesus steps into the midst of our storm and says, "Be not afraid — it is I."

Suddenly, as we hear the calming assurance of His voice, the loose ends of despair come together. Hope binds together what fear has broken. We begin to believe again that we will make it; we can make a difference, and we can truly walk places that previously would have been impossible.

God Knits You Whole

God knits you whole. He only needs a thread of faith to weave an ending unlike the scripted failures of your past. You may feel that your failures have created a stormy sea in which you will sink, lost in oblivion forever. But God has different plans for you.

In the midst of your sinking moment, reach out. Feel the firm grip of God's caring hand. That is a hand that weaves through the emotional waves of tragedy and fear, stitching the black night with golden peace, and covering you with a beautiful garment of joy sewn from the heaviness in your heart.

Without Jesus, you are only partially alive. But at the moment you put your hand in His, or you feel the grasping fingers of grace tugging at you in the swallowing sea, you become connected to the power that makes you whole.

So don't let what just happened to you this week keep you from stepping out in faith, reaching for the impossible dream. Take the step, knowing that if you only make it part of the way, God's helping hand will be there to guide you the entire way.

Chapter Fifteen

Persistence

Everyone knows that an integral part of Christmas is picking out the Christmas tree. My experience in picking out a tree one winter, a few years back, was a lesson in perseverance and good humor. I approached the tree lot confidently, a self-professed cedar and pine expert. Numerous trees were stocked within a chain-linked fence at the local grocery store. The night air was crisp, my breath visible in the air. I was wrapped up in several layers of clothing, topped off by my trusty down jacket. I pulled up in my truck and parked a few feet away from the massive collection of trees.

I shoved my hands in my coat pockets and began inspecting the trees, searching hurriedly for that perfect, pyramidal-shaped tree that would have the honor of standing in our living room for the next month. I found it in less than five minutes. Of course, being a man, eager to get the job done, I felt this was more than enough time to make a decision. I loaded up the pine-scented marvel and headed back to my house, a mere two blocks away.

I arrived to a scene of excited children and a ready-to-decorate mommy. They laughed and played while I struggled through the front door with the "load of cheer." Pine needles fell liberally on the hardwood floor. I set the tree in its circular pedestal and stepped back to observe my 15-minute work of art. Uh-oh!

"It's too short," announced my wife, much to my chagrin.

Suddenly, my smile of confidence dissolved. What did I do next? You guessed it. Aggravated, I took the tree down and shoved it through the front door, leaving another trail of pine needles in its wake. This was only the start of a night of unparalleled frustration in the world of Christmas tree hunting.

I headed back to the store, with less enthusiasm this time. I tossed the rejected tree back in the spot where I had found it. Looking around for its replacement, I suddenly feasted my eyes upon the "perfect" tree. I snatched it up, hurled it in the truck, and spun out for home. My throat had developed an irritating tickle, no doubt brought on by my aggravation, and I found myself clearing my throat more with each passing minute.

I wheeled into the driveway, quickly parked, and roughly grabbed the tree. Then I went through the same ritual: dragging the tree through the door, raining pine needles everywhere, setting it in place, and standing back, waiting for my wife's approval.

This time the tree was too tall. The top was bent against the ceiling, giving it a lopsided appearance that just wasn't acceptable to the Christmas perfectionist standing next to me. Now, I would have come up with a clever way of saying how unique it was and call it a night. But, as you now know, I was not living in some cave with a club and a primitive wife. Things had to change. I went back to the store.

Upon my third entry into the house with a Christmas tree, I was clearing my throat, gritting my teeth and humming with frustration, "O Christmas tree, O Christmas tree, how ugly are thy branches..."

I set the tree in place with the precision of a tree-erecting professional and stepped back to admire it. My face fell. In my rush to get this ongoing event over with, I had picked out a dead tree. That's right — a lifeless, brown-branched, limb-sagging tree. My family started giggling. And, throwing my hands up, I joined them, overcome with laughter. We chuckled, shook our heads in disbelief, and then I headed back to the store again.

By then, it was my fourth trip to the store, the temperature outside had dropped a few more degrees, and my back was aching. You would think, by now, that I would have learned my lesson. Be patient. Choose carefully. But not me. Reaching quickly for the next green victim of this twilight zone experience, I thought again how wonderful it would be to just have an artificial tree. I took the fourth tree back to the house. Drug it through the door. Set it up. Stood back and smiled.

This poor tree had scoliosis. The bottom of the tree was about six inches out of alignment with the top. Even my little kids were shaking their heads by now, thinking, "Dad, how hard can it be to pick out a Christmas tree?!"

My wife, overwhelmed by my ineptitude, hopped in the truck with me this time. We drove back to the store. She swiftly surveyed the remaining trees on the lot. And with the keen eye of a genius, she picked out the perfect tree.

Now, as humorous as this story is, it can teach us something about the persistence of grace. Just as my wife wanted to get the right tree, enduring the comical traverse back and forth to the store, so God endures the many times we make poor choices. He patiently waits for that one moment when every drop of blood He shed for us pays off.

Now, if something as trivial as a Christmas tree is worth pursuing, how much more will God's mercy linger for the treasure of a soul? While the first part of this chapter was aimed at provoking a little laughter, or at least a mild chuckle, the recent episodes of your life may be nothing to smile about at all.

Maybe you've been trying to get someone to love you for a long time.

Maybe you've explored the same territory of anger over and over again — and every time you get the same result.

Maybe you've dreamed of a better job. So you work harder and sleep less, trying to reach your goal. But the more you try, the more trying your circumstances. That job is still caught in the web of impossibility, and the spider of despair is slowly sucking the life out of your dream.

Maybe you've seen your 15th marriage counselor. You've tried to change, but you keep stumbling over your pride, and the gap between you and your spouse is growing.

Maybe you've been to see yet another doctor, hoping for a cure for your disease. And you've gotten so used to wagging heads, ineffective prescriptions, and cordial shrugs, you are expecting this final doctor to respond in the same way.

If any of these scenarios ring true to you, let me encourage you to persist. If the door is slammed in your face, try the window. If the bridge is burned out ahead, build a boat. If the accuser is screaming at you, open your mouth and shout to God.

Whatever you do, don't give up. I know that is a simple, overused slogan of positive thinking, but when you are winded on the uphill path, ready to faint and let the vultures of cynicism eat you alive, what is it you need to hear the most? "Don't give up!" Don't surrender your dream to the dragon of impossibility. You can slay that dragon with persistence.

———•◦•———

In Luke 11, Jesus shares with His listeners a parable of an importunate friend. This friend bombards his best buddy in the middle of the night, while the lights are extinguished, snores fill the air, and even the dogs are stretched out in death-like sleep. But an incessant pounding on the door awakens the owner. The owner discovers that it's his good friend from down the street.

"What do you want?"

"I have a guest who just came into town," the neighbor replies. "I have nothing to feed him. Can you lend me some bread?"

Nowadays, our response would probably be, "Are you kidding? You got me up in the middle of the night to ask for a loaf of bread? I thought your house had burned down or maybe thieves had ransacked your place — but you just want some bread?"

But Jesus shows us the power of persistence in Luke 11:8:

Persistence

I say unto you, Though he will not rise and give him, because he is his friend, yet because of his importunity he will rise and give him as many as he needeth.

The persistence brought assistance. Jesus then went on to say,

Ask, and it shall be given you; seek, and ye shall find; knock, and it shall be opened unto you (v.9).

So if you have asked and nothing happens, move forward. Keep seeking. And if you seek and nothing happens, be persistent. Knock at the door. Because I believe your relationship with God will cause grace to open the door. It may not be quickly, but He will answer.

Chapter Sixteen

Red Sea Emotions
(Exodus 12-14)

Millions of Hebrews departed Egypt. Freed from slavery, like the azure morning was free of clouds, they traveled with great excitement. The promised land was their destination. Four hundred and thirty years spent in hard labor, constructing another nation's dreams, had not squelched their hopes of independence, of returning to the homeland of Abraham, Isaac, and Jacob.

Moses led the children of Israel through the wilderness. They trudged over bumpy terrain. The crinkled, red ridges of the panoramic view seemed dangerously uninviting, the rouge-colored clay unfriendly to the long lines marching its paths. Its serpentine gulleys were ready to overflow with turbulent waters. Some of the crevices were shaped like sinister eyes, appearing as if the ancient hills were watching the Israelites' every move. Soon, the people came to the Red Sea.

The sea impeded their progress, like a liquid stop sign at the beginning of their journey. The waves and mysterious moans of the deep frightened the Hebrews. They felt trapped, like animals about to be slaughtered, their carcasses left for the carrion birds of the desert. And the wind drifting off the mouth of the sea carried the fetid breath of rotting fish and other foul odors. Their pilgrimage had come to a dead end.

The Red Sea is normally greenish-blue, but occasionally algae grow in the water. When they die, the sea becomes reddish-brown, thus giving it its name. It extends 1,350 miles, from the Indian Ocean to the Suez Gulf. It is over 7,200 feet deep, and more than 100 miles wide in places. It is considered to be one of the hottest and saltiest bodies of water in the world. And on that particular day, in a story replayed throughout time, it would come to be known as the "red sea" for a very different reason.

Pharaoh, having learned of the Israelites' entrapment by the sea, set his face toward the people of God. His malevolent countenance burned with a furnace of hatred, his deep-set eyes appearing like pinholes of fire in a cave. He gave the command, and 600 chariots dashed forth. The horses moved swiftly, nostrils flared, ears pinned back, heads moving in the furious rhythm of war. They kicked up clouds of dirt. Snapped tree branches lay in their tumultuous wake. Hooves thundered on the rocky trail like drumbeats, accompanied by the sound of the riders' lashing whips. Soon, they converged upon the dismayed Hebrews. Capture seemed imminent.

The Israelites caught wind of the oncoming armies of Pharaoh. They heard the shrill revolutions of chariot wheels grinding in the sand, inching ever closer to apprehend them and take them back to the whip and the perpetual circles of mill work in Pharaoh's cities. Panic moved in where peace had so recently resided. The people stood with wide eyes, mouths open in silent cries of terror. Their hearts pounded, internal prisoners demanding to be set free from rib cages. Their worst nightmare had shown up and snatched away the short-lived bliss of their promised land dreams. The whole scene became one of chaos: mothers jerking up toddlers, infants crying, elders gasping at the shock, and young warriors clutching their swords for one last stand.

Some began to murmur, voicing their suspicions that Moses had lead them out of Egypt to die in the desert because there were not enough gravesites in Egypt.

How often do we turn the sanctuary into a cemetery, a place where unbelief buries our hopes and dreams? We make God's house a dead requiem instead of a burgeoning revival.

Only a few hours earlier, everything had seemed to be in their favor. The sun was cordial, a golden dial of peaceful rays, the wind a gentle breeze scented with the aroma of daisies. And the temperature was mild, pleasantly endurable for the journey. But now, in the face of unexpected adversity, the sun seemed annoyingly bright, the wind gusted with gritty sand that bit into weary faces, and even the temperature seemed unbearably hot, conjuring up sticky sweat and glistening beads of fear on furrowed brows.

Because of sudden waves of trouble, the contented became the contentious.

Fear's Interpretation

Fear has a way of making us reinterpret the normal events of our lives, reversing our opinions of what is good or bad. Supports transform into hideous repellents.

Friends become foes. One molehill doesn't just turn into a mountain, but into an entire range of antagonism. Every shadow has a monster as its source. Every spoken word has a hidden meaning, intended to knock us off balance, to condemn or shame us.

Fear revisits forgotten shame. New problems torment the fragile arenas of our faith. We remember the worst — bruises of rejection, scars of broken relationships, wounds of abuse, tender spots of addiction, injuries of gossip, and lonely sunsets of grief. Fear dredges up the debris buried in our memories, and then we feel we have to deal with those memories all over again. It becomes a vicious cycle of two steps forward and three steps back, until we feel stranded in routine guilt. No need to even go forward anymore because we've learned what comes next. It becomes a dark faith in bad outcomes. Optimistic mornings become pessimistic afternoons that flow into nightmarish evenings; and then comes the dawn of a new day, ready for yet more disappointment.

"Fear hath torment..." (I John 3:18). The word "torment" means "penal infliction" — a not-yet-served sentence of guilt. When the Egyptians showed up, intending to recapture the Israelites, it caused God's people to think negatively because the wounds of slavery were still very fresh.

Unexpected changes in circumstances are like sudden changes in weather, where blue skies can turn turbulently black in a matter of minutes. That is what the Red Sea became for Israel — a sudden change in the weather of expectation that took their hopes of a brighter future and swallowed them in the swirling seas of impossibility.

Moses, unflinching in his resolve, stood upon a pulpit of rock and encouraged the fear-stricken mass. His robes spread out like wings in the gusty wind.

> *Fear ye not, stand still, and see the salvation of the LORD, which he will shew to you today: for the Egyptians whom ye have seen today, ye shall see them again no more for ever. The LORD shall fight for you, and ye shall hold your peace* (Exodus 14:13-14).

Faith's Intervention

Having received his instructions from God, Moses stretched out the anointed staff over the sea. And "all that night" God caused an east wind to divide the waters. What is God working on during your night? While the darkness steals sight from you, clouding your vision, God could be paving a new path in the midst of impossibility. So, don't look at the night, a season of blinded comprehension, as a waste of time. It may very well be a work of treasure, a time when God is forming a passage of deliverance during the darkness.

Israel marched over the sea on dry ground. There were two walls of water, twin aquariums, bordering the escaping Hebrews. God had made an incision in the Red Sea, and soon, this miracle would turn out to be Egypt's greatest wound. The journey across filled the people with mixed emotions — hesitant smiles, suspicious eyes, cautious strides followed by hurried steps, wary elders peering over their shoulders. But the closer the people came to the rising slope of the other side, the more their cowardice waned and confidence marked their faces.

Then God removed the fiery barrier. The 10,000 Egyptians, stubborn to the end, ventured to follow the fleeing Jews. And, once again, the Israelites felt dread overtake them. First they thought they were getting away, but then saw the approaching chariots. God divided the sea, they marched almost all the way over without incident, and then they thought, *Here come those relentless chariots again.*

(How well I can relate to this vacillating ride of victory and defeat! One minute, I feel 10,000 miles removed from poor attitudes or reactions from my past. And then, boom! Here come those chariots of anger, or bitterness, or self-pity. Will I ever get rid of them?)

Within a matter of minutes, the scene changed dramatically. God reached down with invisible hands, knocked out the props holding up the walls of water, and then death came out to paint the sea crimson.

Soon there were dead Egyptian soldiers everywhere; pale cadavers floated on the sea; waves bumped lifeless bodies toward the shore; water seeped from gaping mouths; eyes were sightless, staring into infinite darkness. Chariots clinked in the water against the rocky bluffs. A macabre feast of Pharaoh's men lay on the soggy sands awaiting the descent of the gathering vultures. Pharaoh found out the hard way that the Red Sea was not a trap for Israel, but for God's enemies.

On the opposite shore, where astonished Israelites witnessed the slaughter, the pendulum of emotions swung back to joy. Cheering mothers and daughters danced, jingling tambourines, while men leapt in relief at the miracle.

Faith in Transition

You may believe, at times, that your dreams are beyond reach. In the transitional phases of life — high school to college, singleness to marriage, married couple to married with kids — you may feel unnoticed, ineffective, and neglected. But the passage through your Red Sea is like being in a cocoon of character. It becomes of place of development, not delay. Sometimes you want to stretch against the gauzy fabric of faith, break out of the confines, and be free. But I encourage you to stay in the process. Don't rush God's timing. When you get through this transitional phase, you will be able to look back and see God's perfect wisdom.

> *Yea, though I walk through the valley of the shadow of death, I will fear no evil: for thou art with me; thy rod and thy staff they comfort me* (Psalm 23:4).

David shares with us his confidence in God. I believe he has no fear because he is focused. His lens of faith zooms in on the rod and staff of protection. When I see the protection of God, I do not have to fear the predators of hell. They may come after me with false accusations, morbid remembrances of failure, instant replays of unkindness to someone or by someone; but if I truly keep focused on the Shepherd, I will be secure, and those disquieting symptoms will flee. For they are sure to come, those hounds of suspicion, wolves of distrust, and hungry lions of carnal indignation.

But His rod and staff comfort me, just as Moses comforted the apprehensive Israelites at the Red Sea. When the way seemed inescapable and the odds of returning to slavery undeniable, God inspired the man of God to raise his staff. For the people, the staff — which symbolized the authority of God — must also have been an anchor of hope, a mainstay that triggered belief in the impossible every time it was raised.

Think of this: the cross of Christ is like Moses' staff raised high over the sea. His cross, although bloody and grotesque, authored peace for you. So the next time you feel fear rushing in like the Egyptians, look to the cross. See it as a shepherd's staff erected over your troubled waters. You will make it through. And some day soon, when you look back on the transition from trouble to triumph, you will be able to say with the psalmist, "Yea, though I walk through the valley...." (Psalm 23:4). You will make it to the other side.

Chapter Seventeen

Fixing Leaks

Iremember, as a child, roofing with my dad. I sat on the ridge and slid shingles to him. He fastened them to the roof with a staple gun. The chicaty-chicaty-chicaty sound of the gun sliding over the shingles, inserting the staples with the pull of a trigger, could be mesmerizing. At times it seemed like my dad kept time with an invisible band playing on the ridge. Every few minutes, as if on cue, the rumbling compressor on the ground provided the bass section, sounding like a long, drawn out trombone score. Air generated through the snaking hoses, hissing where clamps weakened. We worked with an entire orchestra of sounds.

I enjoyed the sweaty, long hours of work in the summer furnace of day. I seldom wore a hat but let the sun rays bronze my face and arms. And the occasional breeze made me shudder in my sweat-drenched shirt; I'd pretend I just dove into a deep, icy-cold pool. Roofing in the dehydrating heat brought about a deep thirst. A vigorous swig from the watercooler during breaks was more than refreshing — it was revitalizing.

Carrying bundles of shingles strengthened my legs, which later benefited me on the basketball court, enabling me to jump higher. Granules avalanched with each grating step toward the ridge. The shingles we used consisted of a three-in-one tab made predominately of rough fiberglass, good for scratching an itch, bad for sliding on with thin clothing. My dad would bandage his fingertips in tape to keep them from getting raw while handling the shingles.

Sometimes I slipped while carrying a bundle of shingles, and I would scrape my elbows against their abrasive surface. The knees of my work pants never lasted very long, because dragging my knees on the roof had a sandpaper effect. Before long, holes appeared, and around the frayed edges, tiny threads fluttered in the wind. I would come home looking like Huckleberry Finn. All I needed was a raft and the Mississippi River.

Sometimes in the sweltering heat, the roof turned into a skillet on which you could cook an egg. In the winter the shingles were brittle, but in the summer they were soft and flimsy, like giant sticks of chewing gum.

At the end of most work days, there was an acrid fragrance of rain-scented shingles, tar buckets, sweaty clothes, melted, uneaten peanut butter and jelly sandwiches, and honeysuckle in the air. Heading home, I always knew there would be no need for imaginary sheep arcing over my bed that night. I would need no tricks to induce sleep because it would come quickly and deeply.

My dad kept roofing materials around the house, often stacked on wooden crates. My keen imagination transformed loose shingles into imaginary soldiers, and sometimes the front yard would be scattered with torn shingles, acting as decapitated casualties of war. Mom and Dad didn't particularly share my enthusiasm for the props used in these epic battle scenes. After all, I was the general, and petty cleanup was for someone else. But my dad firmly explained to me that the old shingles were all right for horseplay, but not the new ones.

For my dad, roofing was a way of making a living, a means to pay bills and enjoy a few modest pleasures in life. But the lessons learned from the hard labor of roofing go beyond money. For me, they apply to ministry, as well (maybe the Lord truly has called me to the "shingles" ministry!).

I learned at a young age why adequate roofing was so important. If you didn't have a good roof, you might not only enjoy the sound of the tapping rain in your living room, but the feel of it, as well. First, it would start out as tiny droplets and then widen into a stream. And finally, there would probably be a torrential downpour pouring all over your furniture.

You can have a beautiful, spacious, expensive home, but if the roof leaks, the fancy mural on the wall, the ornate coffered ceiling, the plush carpet, and precious artifacts within the home all stand a good chance of being ruined. Good roofing is less about aesthetics and more about keeping inclement weather on the outside. Leakage can destroy precious keepsakes. Leakage can ruin the inner structure of older homes. Leakage can ruin priceless family photos.

You may not own a mansion. You may not live in a beach house, surrounded by squawking sea gulls. You may not dwell in a ranch house on endless acres of land. But even if you simply own a two-room shanty, you still want a roof that doesn't leak.

A functional roof is much like the protective covering of authority. Careless living leaves the heart vulnerable to wounding sorrows. The disobedient man has no roof over his head; he is open to the elements of evil inventions. Submission to godly leadership provides protection, much like a shield.

A ministry without an effective covering creates the possibility of damaging leaks — leaks of character...unwanted springs of pride...discouraging drips of doubt...tearstains of regret...waterfalls of malice...downpours of disappointment.

> *Obey them that have the rule **over you**, and **submit** yourselves: for they watch for your souls, as they that must give account, that they may do it with joy, and not with grief: for that is unprofitable for you* (Hebrews 13:17 emphasis mine).

I key on the words *over* and *submit* in relation to a covering or roof. Storms of deception can be avoided if one listens to the wise voices of the ministry. Their loving instructions work like a strong roof, tightly fitted, leaving no cracks to be exploited by unhealthy thoughts. There are a lot of things I may feel are important, areas I'm passionate about, but if I submit them to caring, older men, I may discover flaws I wasn't aware of. Without God-fearing submission, I could develop spiritual dementia — obsessions of the heart that can no longer distinguish between right and wrong. I know that may sound extreme, but many have become self-destructive because they wouldn't listen to godly counsel. They tore off the roof of security, and ungodly opinions formed like dark clouds, raining confusion on their perceptions.

Submission guards my ambition; it shields me from displeasing desires that threaten my walk with God. When I think of the outward elements that can harm my mind and wreak havoc on my values — those that are established through my relationship with God — I think of three particular things: The lust of the flesh, the lust of the eyes, and the pride of life. These are perils to my conscience, the way I perceive life, and the pursuit of God's standard of excellence.

Submission protects honorable tradition. As stated earlier, an older home may be replete with antique furniture and irreplaceable, sentimental artifacts. These things are like our time-tested spiritual traditions, such as prayer and fasting, daily devotion in the Word of God, caring for the less fortunate.

Submission keeps me from decomposition. Decomposition is the breaking up of constituent parts; it is a decaying process. Many convictions decay over time because the roof of submission leaks. Little by little the walls of faith erode, the once fresh paint of love fades into tarnished loathing, and the clocks of faithfulness no longer tick due to an accumulation of moisture.

You can always tell where a roof has been leaking. The ceiling will have a rusty stain, as if someone has opened too many shaken cans of soda, and the effervescent geyser sprayed on that one area. Roofs tend to leak around pipes. Maybe in our case the leakage of pride and the destruction of submission begin in our own "set of pipes" — our voices. We say the wrong things by uttering insensitive comments and interjecting our own vehement biases.

My dad was called out on occasion to repair a roof after a storm. Most of the leaks showed up in the valleys, near pipes, or in the intersecting levels of a house. The similarities are amazing, when compared to the places where tribulations occur in life. Where do most of our problems occur? Do we not say in the valley, or in relationships because of what was said, or in trying to reach the next level of ministry or faith?

We usually repaired the leaking areas of a roof with tar, or a metal lining called "flashing." It wasn't necessary to demolish the whole house, wipe the foundation clean, and rebuild from scratch. Sometimes it only took 30 minutes for the problem to be fixed, the leak stopped, and the homeowners made secure about protecting against future leaks. If only we could learn the same lesson about the power of prayer! Instead of pushing the panic button by demolishing our relationships, wouldn't it be better to spend a few minutes in prayer? The hot tar of prayer fixes most leaks in our faith. We just have to be willing to take the time to determine the leaky areas, and then take the necessary steps to mend it.

Submit yourselves therefore to God. Resist the devil, and he will flee from you (James 4:7).

Notice submission precedes resistance. We have no power to resist the devil if we do not submit all the areas of our lives to God. The enemy of truth, the master manipulator of human emotion and will, comes at a weakened spirit with great storms of confusion. You hear people say, "When it rains, it pours," often meaning that nothing is working out right, or one bad thing after another is happening. Those are the vulnerable times for the child of God because he may be tempted to seek inferior alternatives or compromises to solve his problems. The hardest time to submit to God is when we feel violated by someone or something that was said. We want to take matters into our own hands, and give someone the five-fold ministry in the form of a fist.

But if we make ourselves amenable to God's plan, He will cover us with His love. In our humility we will find a secure shield from anger, strife and vengeance. Forgiveness repairs our minds and keeps out intrusive grudges. It is not always easy to turn the other cheek, and often I have resorted to arguing to prove a point. But I have found, in most instances, that this just damages my "spiritual roof," allowing leaks of stress and even sleeplessness to seep through.

I can deflate my woes when I prostrate my will. "Not my will, but thine be done" makes for a glib cliché, but it means more to God when I perform, not just profess, the words. In roofing, I learned that shingles work best when they're not "stuck up," but when they lay flat. In the same way, I work best when my attitudes are humbly stretched out on the altar, flattened to the floor in tearful intercession, and not raised up in quarrelsome debate.

You may have several leaks in your spiritual life. You may feel they are so numerous that it is impossible to fix. Leaks are often simple signs of neglect. What area of your life have you neglected to submit to God? Start there. I am sure you will not only locate the leaks, but you will also know how to repair them.

Chapter Eighteen

Fast-Forward Faith

Receiving the end of your faith, even your salvation.
(I Peter 1:9)

Have you ever felt like someone pushed the pause button on your life, leaving you stranded in purposelessness? We all go through times when it seems the momentary delays of life will turn into long-term disappointments. Maybe we've stopped short of our dreams because we're burned-out and burdened with excessive demands. We feel that we are destined to fail and that the ambitions seeded deep in our spirits will never flourish.

Spiritual desires can become distant sounds lost in the high decibel world of demanding jobs and hollow journeys. You hold your life's aspirations like a tiny cassette tape in the palm of your hand, ready to play out each scene, anticipating the fulfillment of every one of them. But as you are playing your tape of dreams, click! The pause button is pressed, and everything is put on hold.

Peace is put on hold because of an unexpected trauma. Forgiveness is suspended due to the perpetual betrayal of a loved one.

Perhaps your master's degree gets slotted in the wish-I-could-have-done-that file because a loved one requires your daily care. Or maybe your children grow through all the stages of their lives, and you miss much of it because the I'm-gonna-be-home-more-often promises got tucked away in the good intention drawer when the boss said you had to travel more often.

Ambitions can be suspended, dreams delayed, intentions dulled, and life-long goals postponed indefinitely.

The idea of fast-forward faith lies in the power of the prophetic. God, at times, lifts us above the storms and adversities that war against our dreams so we can reach the end result: the completion of our spiritual objectives.

Like a man caught in a terrible storm offshore, you are now able to see the path of salvation, the moment of deliverance even before it comes because of your deep trust in God. You know you will make it to the shore of your destiny, not because of an inflated ego, but because you're humbly relying on God's promises. This knowledge is not based on mere premonition, but on the security of your faith in God, allowing you to access strength even in the midst of weakness and vulnerability. Distractions may thunder, but your destiny will thrive.

The apostle Paul, in Acts 27, insured the lives of everyone on board his ship before the storm hit because he had been visited by an angel of the Lord. The shimmering presence of God's ethereal messenger stood by his bedside, and while Paul rubbed the sleep from his eyes, trying to discern between dreams and reality, the angel spoke. He told Paul that he would stand before Caesar one day, and that God had given him the lives of every man on board. When the curdling clouds, filled with the sour rain and winds of spoiled weather, spilled across the sky, and the ship became uncontrollable in the churning winds, Paul stood among the people and told them the Word of God. The men were stuck in fear, but *Paul's belief in God's Word gave him fast-forward faith, and with boldness he declared the safety of every man.*

The men threw cargo overboard and watched it bob away in the sea. They went without food for days, becoming weaker every hour from malnourishment and dehydration. Bloodshot eyes drooped, and the men seemed ready to collapse at any moment. But Paul knew God's Word would not fail.

The fiery lights of the night sky were extinguished by smothering clouds, and the sun turned a blind eye toward their predicament. But Paul trusted God's course; he had seen the angelic light at the end of the storm's tunnel. After three days, when everything weighting the ship down had been tossed overboard, each citizen of this new precinct of terror seemed ready to make their permanent home at the bottom of the sea. But Paul had spoken; the prophecy had gone forth; the divine oracle was set.

The men were now sick, vomiting up what little was left in their stomachs, feverish, their bodies seeming to wage war against nature's forces. They held their stomachs and moaned in fear as the storm hit them with its fiercest attack. Still, Paul remained confident. Even though he knew the ship would be shattered when it ran aground and was pounded by the surf, he believed that God was still with him in this impossibility zone, and with all the other men who stayed with the ship.

At one point during the storm, some of the men tried to sneak off the ship in a lifeboat. Paul intervened, warning them that safety was found on the ship, not on the high seas of mutiny. In the same way, we can't leave the Church when trouble comes. If we stay loyal to the people of God, we'll be safe; for even if the building is destroyed, the Body of Christ is indestructible. Stay loyal to the vision. Remain with the people of God, no matter how impossible the circumstances may seem. For if God has spoken victory before the storm, then we know the outcome and we will overcome.

———•◆•———

Fast-forward faith is better than slow, going-in-reverse fear or breathless neutral. Being stuck in neutral is somewhat like death. You just can't move. You can have the best-looking sailboat, fixed with the most elaborate sails, engineered by the smartest builders, but if the wind doesn't blow, it isn't going to move. In the same way, you have to have the Spirit of God, the wind of truth, blowing in order to get a church moving. Often we are stuck in neutral, our sails limp and boat stalled, because we are trying to get things moving with human will and ingenuity alone.

Faith puts things in proper perspective. When we trust the Lord, He breathes on our waters of desire, and the sails of our dreams become taut with the steady wind of His blessing. We are able to move forward. And while the wind may blow us in any direction, we have the assurance that wherever the wind takes us, it is the direction we are supposed to go.

Fast-forward faith requires relying on the wind of God's will. We need to be humble and submit our desires and ambitions to the perfect guidance of His Spirit. Our direction will never be as good or accurate as the direction God wants us to go. We may be tempted to fire up humanistic engines, pull down the sails, and just motor our way to whatever shore our heart desires, but we will never be as fulfilled as when we let the wind of God lead us. Only God knows the perfect plan for our lives. We can't get so caught up in the hot air of our own aspirations that we end up blowing ourselves off course.

———•—•———

In Genesis, Esau blew himself off course by cranking up the engines of self-appeasement. Gratification robbed him of grace. Momentary satisfaction emptied his sea of God's blessing. He became stranded on an island of despair, unable to reclaim the birthright taken from him by his own brother. Esau didn't go forward because he lived his life in the shallows of earthly need, while heavenly destiny blew on by. His sails were tangled up in satisfying his desire for an aromatic bowl of beans.

In II Kings, Gehazi set sail on the sea of his own reward. He tracked down Naaman after his master, Elisha, had sent him off, declining his generous offerings of gold and fancy garments. But Gehazi hurried into the reckless sea of self-appointment. He ignored the forecast of his conscience and sailed into the dangerous waters of disobedience. And soon, his prophetic calling sank in the deep waters of treachery. Oh, he got his bags of silver and fine threads spun at the finest silk shops, but he lost his future in the process.

If he could have encountered a fast-forward faith moment, perhaps he could have transcended the temptation and envisioned a better day when he would receive a double portion of Elisha's spirit; when he, like Elisha in the shadow of Elijah, would have watched the wind-rippled mantle float down upon his own shoulders. But he got stuck in the sea with no wind, his sails drooping, his ministry drowned by unbelief.

We can all avoid these mistakes if we look through the periscope of God's Word to see that trusting Him is what will move us toward our destiny.

Benefits of Fast-Forward Faith

It Helps Cure Ailing Confidence. When you are able to get a glimpse of where God is taking you and what His ultimate plan for your life is, it boosts your confidence. It's better than a B-12 injection. It energizes you and gives you the internal fortitude to remain calm in stressful times. You know God's calling on your life is definite, you've seen the fruit of that calling in dreams, you walk the path of discipline to see it come to pass, so you're able to maintain composure even in the whirlwinds of disappointment and setbacks.

Impossibilities just stimulate your resolve when you've been to the mountain and you've seen the promised land. Your attitude is not one of arrogance. You do not speak pridefully, alienating others in God's Kingdom. But you do have a quiet, deep assurance in your heart that what God has placed you on earth to do will be done.

It Helps You Conclude Unfinished Tasks. You look at

the blueprints of your dream. Dust has collected in numerous creases; it has been folded up many times and tucked away. At times you may have started building its foundation. A few framed walls lean together in the wind. But then disappointment, frustration, and depleted motivation took over. You put the plans away. Then your fast-forward faith kicks in the moment you envision the fulfilled dream.

You are now ready to finish what fear has delayed. You put on the nail apron and go to work on the unfinished areas, hammering nails into the framework of your dream, fastening doors on hinges of hope, placing windows into the open spaces that once contained the coolness of doubt.

> Now you can finish that degree.
> Now you can go on that missions trip.
> Now you can start that new business.
> Now you can finish writing that book.
> Now you can love that person no one else wants to deal with.

Now. Now. Now. Because you have seen God's hand interlace with yours, you can trade "no" for "now!" Go ahead. Start finishing what you had finished believing in.

It Helps You Construct Resistance Against Temptation. Lastly, I believe fast-forward faith helps you construct a firewall of resistance against temptation. When you've had a chance to see the gold in the mountain of God's tomorrow, you won't settle for the dusty copper of sin today. You know that God offers the best. Any other route of earthly satisfaction will only lead you to heart-breaking defeat. Seeing God's Way, knowing His provisional course, and deciding to choose it over hell's shortcut is as simple as knowing that a fountain's water will taste better than the cesspool's.

Heaven is a real place. The fairy tales of human philosophy cannot compare to the actual place where sin will cease, death will die, the grave will be buried, and peace will be the order of the eternal day.

Chapter Nineteen

What Are You Praying For?

And forthwith Jesus gave them leave. And the unclean spirits went out, and entered into the swine: and the herd ran violently down a steep place into the sea, (they were about two thousand;) and were choked in the sea. And they that fed the swine fled, and told it in the city, and in the country. And they went out to see what it was that was done. And they come to Jesus, and see him that was possessed with the devil, and had the legion, sitting, and clothed, and in his right mind: and they were afraid. And they that saw it told them how it befell to him that was possessed with the devil, and also concerning the swine. And they began to pray him to depart out of their coasts (Mark 5:13-17).

When the sun sank, the terror began. It started with frantic running, a tormented figure zigzagging in and out of the tombs. Gray slivers of clouds moved over the bottom half of the moon; fitting ambiance for a night of horror. The wind howled among the rocks and sounded, at times, like inhuman whispers from another world.

The man on the run was scantily clad in torn robes

stained with animal blood and human drool. He looked like a hideous, crossbred beast from earth and hell. His eyes were windows into a demonic world. His beard was ragged, torn away in several places, revealing scabs of old injuries and leaking punctures of new ones. His nose was crooked, having been broken several times while writhing in the grip of demonic possession. If another human had gazed on this monstrosity in the night, they would have been sickened by the sight of his contorted features. For often, his face was twisted up in a dreadful grimace. Bellowing incantations from the nether regions, his unintelligible words echoed torment from the suffering beings of eternal darkness. This was none other than the "madman of Gadara."

Gadara was a city of many luxuries, known as a chief city of the Decapolis during Roman times. It was the capital of the Roman province of Peraea, and was located east of Jordan, about six miles south of the Sea of Galilee. It was known for its basilica baths, large theaters and, especially, a central street lined with columns. It was against a backdrop of hills, stone-carved sarcophagi, and colonnades of cedars that the madman lurked. Few were brave enough to explore the caves where he camped. On several occasions, various groups of people had attempted to put chains on him, but he was too strong to contain, and would angrily snap the chains in a display of superhuman strength.

Every day at twilight, mothers would hurriedly gather their young children from the foothills, ordering them to the safety of guarded homes and locked doors. Grown men could be seen standing at the edge of town with torches, waving them back and forth, carefully scanning the tree line of the forest to make sure the madman was not in sight. But even if they didn't see him, they could hear him. His wolfish howling sent shivers down the spines of Gadara's inhabitants. And they often wondered: how long would they have to fear violence from the madman?

But from across the sea came a man of love and compassion. He discerned the writhing demons in men's souls and could deliver them. Jesus stepped off the boat and sank His sandals in the soft sand. The confrontation took place within a matter of minutes. The startled disciples looked up to see a beastly figure dashing toward the Messiah. He threw himself at the feet of Jesus.

Jesus recognized instantly what tormented this man and said with undaunted authority, "Come out of this man, you evil spirit!" (v. 8).

As the man moaned, his body gave off a putrid odor of uncleanness. His body perspired profusely and drenched his garments with sweat. He rocked back and forth on bruised knees and began to worship the Lord. Unseen to the natural eye were the tangled, serpent-like spirits coiled within the man's body. He was used to their hissing, the way they slithered around in his mind, poisoning his thoughts.

But at this moment, they became servile to the stature of Christ. The brightness of Jesus' glory must have shown like the sun to these creatures. For they had been accustomed to darkness, far from the grace of God. There was only one thing they could do now — implore God not to torment them further.

A chorus of demonic voices rose, like the sound of a screaming crowd burning in a fire.

"What do you want with me, Jesus, Son of the Most High God? I implore you by God, do not torment me!" (v.7).

"What is your name?" asked Jesus.

"Legion," growled the innumerable voices of the faceless specters.

"Legion" was a military term applied to principle units of the Roman army. It usually encompassed a company of between 3,000 to 6,000 soldiers, and 100 to 300 cavalrymen. In other words, this man was inhabited by literally thousands of evil spirits.

This legion of demons begged Jesus not to send them out of the area. A herd of pigs could be heard snorting and grunting nearby. The demons eyed the mud-coated swine and immediately implored Jesus to cast them into the pigs.

Jesus gazed at the wallowing pigs, slopping around in the wet mud, and probably thought there was not a more fitting home for these intruders from hell. With a flick of His hand, He motioned the demons a farewell bidding into the swine. A vacuuming sound pervaded the spiritual atmosphere around the madman. Like a swarm of flies lifting off one dead body and onto another, the demons winged their way toward the herd of pigs.

Suddenly the man's fingers, which had been gnarled like talons, were straightened and relaxed. His eyes, which had been black like a starless night, were now gleaming. The whites of the eyes were vivid and clear. His face, which moments earlier was bloated and full of pain, was now delicately sculpted with peaceful features. Even his hair, though still filthy, seemed more tame. The "madman" had disappeared. A mild man had replaced him.

Meanwhile, the pigs were going wild. Mud showered in every direction. The rhythm of snorts and grunts intensified. The pigs ran in circles, climbed on the slippery backs of other pigs, rolled frantically on their backs as if trying to get a pail full of leeches off, and rammed into each other, confused. Then, as if an invisible piper appeared at the ledge of the hill, they turned toward the sea and charged. Over the edge they tumbled, spraying the amazed onlookers above with water. In a matter of minutes, the round bellies and pink flesh of the pigs floated lifelessly on the sea of death.

You would think at this moment the citizens of Gadara would be cheering. But there was no rejoicing that day. Although Jesus had cast out a legion of demons, He had also stirred up a hornet's nest. The people were highly displeased that Jesus had caused such an uproar. Even though the man once wild with countless demons now sat before them clothed and in his right mind, they only prayed for one thing: that Jesus would leave. They would rather dine on swine than host the healer.

The demoniac prayed for deliverance from his spiritual prison; the demons prayed for delay of future punishment; and the citizens prayed for Messiah's departure from their premises. Guess what? Jesus accommodated every prayer.

So here you are, living in the impossibility zone of forgotten prayers, burned-out fields of dreams, crushed confidences, and empty feelings. You don't want to pray about certain things anymore because you are tired of getting a negative response or no response at all. But consider this: if Jesus would answer the prayer of a demon, how much more does He desire to answer the prayer of a disciple?

If you've stopped praying a particular prayer because time has yielded no results, you feel inadequate in the presence of God, or because you have failures in your life that stifle your courage to ask God for certain things, have faith. Let this passage renew your confidence, restoring passion to your dormant dreams. Pray about them again. Renew your trust in a God who cares a lot more about you than some pig-seeking demons.

Chapter Twenty

Just a Stone's Throw
From Victory
(I Samuel 17)

David sat among the sheep, his harp cradled in his lap. Soft tufts of grass made for cushioned seating as he played. The sheep curiously flicked their ears on occasion, some playfully bleating as if to provide David with background singers from the animal kingdom. Ticking branches provided momentary percussion as the agreeable wind moved in rhythm with David's songwriting.

A distant storm containing iron black clouds boomed to the east. But there was no threat of rain — the storm would move well beyond the perimeters of the farm. Yet the drumming thunder pleased the harpist; with nature providing the harmony, he had quite a cosmic orchestra to work with.

David was so caught up in his music that he did not hear his father calling him. Then he abruptly stopped playing, at the sound of his father's voice. He jumped up quickly, darted over the little creek like a deer, and ran to the front of the house.

"What is it, Father?" David asked, noticing the troubled look on his father's face.

"You've been singing again, haven't you?" Joseph asked.

"Yes, sir," David replied. "I just wrote a new song. Would you like to hear it?"

He was already poised to sing the first verse. But his father had other things on his mind.

"No, son," he said. "I need you to go to the valley of Elah. Take some bread, cheese, and parched corn to your brothers. Bring me back a report of their welfare."

"Yes, sir."

David stored his harp in a wooden box, grabbed his shepherd's bag, hopped onto the carriage and proceeded to Elah. He bounced along the uneven terrain. When he came within 100 yards of the camp, he pulled the reigns, bringing the carriage to a halt. The carriage rocked back and forth from the abrupt stop. David dismounted, grabbed some of the food, and hurried to find his brothers.

At first, the brothers seemed in good spirits. Then suddenly, as if a shift in the temperature had occurred, their moods changed. Their warmth dissolved, replaced by cold shivers of fear. The chill of death now drove Israel's soldiers further back into the caves. For a moment, all was silent. And then David heard the deafening thunder of a man's voice.

"Israel! Send me a champion to fight. Or are you too afraid?" The man began to hurl insults at Israel's army. And then someone told David his name: Goliath.

Goliath's legs looked like tree trunks. He left footprints behind in the soft ground like a dinosaur. His eyes bulged with anger. He had a scar that ran like lightning down his left cheek, a bearded, squared jaw, and a voice that sounded like distant thunder. The glimmer off his brazen coat of arms blinded those who dared to look at him from the opposite mountain. He walked with long, sweeping strides that initiated a small avalanche of stones.

From that point, until the moment when David stood in the battlefield, time became a racing chariot that carried him through a blur of events. David was filled with righteous indignation at the giant's words. He stood up on a tall precipice, like a preacher addressing a crowd from his pulpit, and called out boldly, "Who is this uncircumcised Philistine that he would defy the armies of the living God?"

After being chafed by his brothers, questioned by the king, and empowered by God with a few smooth stones for battle, David stepped forward to fight.

Chiffon clouds moved across the buttery horizon. The wind blew gently from the east, rustling David's red hair, as if God was breathing upon him with affectionate favor.

When Goliath saw David approaching, he grinned widely and said, "Am I a dog that you come to me with a stick?"

David didn't flinch. He looked the big boy up and down and said with the confidence of ten soldiers, "You come to me with a sword, a spear, and a shield. But I come to you in the name of the Lord. And today I will feed the flesh of Philistines to the fowl of the air and the beasts of the field."

David glanced around. He could already envision the widespread wings of the vultures circling in the sky, their naked red necks quivering in ravenous anticipation of so much flesh. He could see them stretching out their talons to find purchase on the large, meaty chest of his opponent. At the moment, his scavenger friends were settled on some distant rocks, humpbacked, with their long wings folded away, watching impassively. As he watched his towering enemy make the first move, David smiled, winked at a vulture and a clandestine hyena, and stepped forward.

The sound of pebbles crunching beneath David's running, slapping sandals intoned a warrior's cadence. And the grit of the rocks matched the internal fortitude of the teenager. As he ran, David laced the leather thongs of the slingshot between his fingers. He pulled one of the smooth stones from his shepherd's bag and placed it in the tiny pouch of the slingshot. And then he came to an abrupt halt and dug his left foot into the sand.

With lightning speed, he pitched his arm forward, snapped his wrist and released God's ICBM. The little rock, plucked out of a cold riverbed, placed into the leathery pouch of the slingshot in an urgent moment of faith, and launched forward with the velocity of a whirlwind, whistled onward, quickly gaining speed.

The giant leaned forward, squinting his eyes to focus on the little speck speeding toward him. And before he could react, Boom! The rock struck his head with cataclysmic force. The smack sounded like a bat connecting with a fast-pitched baseball in the strike zone. David had indeed hit the sweet spot right in the middle of Goliath's forehead for a victorious, ninth inning home run!

You, like David, are just a stone's throw away from victory. You may be just one more prayer from the fulfillment of a promise; one more step from supernatural breakthrough; one more foot from the financial miracle you've needed; one more praise from empowerment. Don't fall short. Don't let the enemy of your faith scare you into a cave of disbelief.

Go forward. The devil may be feeding your mind the lie that you are too distant from your destiny to keep going. But God is telling you that you are not far. Just pick up your weapon of intercession, step into the valley of impossibility, launch another faith attack on the fears of darkness, and watch God do amazing things for you.

The Destined Rock

We talk a lot about the tenacious faith of David and how he braved overwhelming odds to defeat Goliath. We talk about Goliath and his enormous size, and we're amazed by his stature and the weight of his armor. But what about the rock that hit him in the forehead? That rock was also significant. It was chosen by David and became the instrument used to save Israel from the Philistine enslavement.

David chose the rock that killed Goliath at random from the river, but the Rock that God chose from the sea of men was not a random selection, but a predestined election. The Rock of salvation that saved man from the giants of death, hell, and the grave was the rejected stone, Jesus Christ. He had His name engraved on that Rock since the very foundation of the world.

The Divine Range

When David faced Goliath on the battlefield, he possessed merely a slingshot. But in terms of the distance required to use the slingshot, his choice of weapon turned out to be the safest. Someone with a sword would have had to get within striking distance of the enemy, exposing himself to the larger, sharper, and more devastating swipe of Goliath's sword. By staying out of the danger zone of Goliath's expertise, David was able to rely on God for the accuracy of the stone.

Often, we go "too far" in our fleshly attempts to fix a matter. We end up saying the wrong thing, going to the wrong place, or getting too much of the credit that rightfully belongs to God. Sometimes we just need to keep our distance and let God do the delivering; let the Rock do the rest. Once David released the stone, the only thing left to do was to wait for the result. In the same way, when you have given counsel or taken a stand, the only thing left to do is wait patiently on God to see where the "stone" finds its mark.

The Defenseless Region

The stone sank into the forehead of the giant. He stood with his bronze coat of mail, bronze greaves, a spear with an iron spearhead, and a huge sword. Yet the stone struck him in the forehead. Even with all his protective armor, Goliath was still vulnerable.

Similarly, a person may surround himself with materialism, the armor of wealth that makes him appear invincible. But every man is vulnerable in some area. Often, that vulnerable spot is in the same place as Goliath's: the area of the mind. As described in

Ephesians chapter 6, we need the helmet of salvation to keep our minds safe.

Being "just a stone's throw from victory" means you're really close to victory, to a change of heart and mind. Reach up and touch your temples. Massage them a little (now don't fall asleep on me). Right there in your head is where victory is found; the place where you can burn memories of God's mercy and grace that guard against all doubt and fear.

Chapter Twenty-One

Continue

Jesus said in John 8:31-32, "If ye continue in my word, then are ye my disciples indeed; And ye shall know the truth, and the truth shall make you free."

The real power of Christianity is found when we make a conscious choice to persevere and continue on our path. Growth is dependent upon this decision. Some miss the ocean of their triumph because they stop paddling in the river of struggle; they get out before God is finished with their journey.

The first part of this verse talks about knowing the truth. Some people only understand this part. They are informed about God. They comprehend the truth of Scripture and its life-changing concepts. But what good is knowledge if passion doesn't also exist? What you know and what you do with that knowledge are dependent upon continuing on your journey. Don't just learn; live what you learn!

If information is all we have, it's not enough. We have to read the second part of the verse: "And the truth shall make you free." That speaks of more than just head knowledge; it talks about true, heartfelt change.

Continue to the Finish

I may be running up a hill, knowing that at the top is a pristine pool of water to refresh my soul, a bucket of gold to enrich my life, and a grand view to excite my spirits. But if I lose the desire to press on the last 300 yards, what good is the knowledge of what waits for me? I will not experience it if I give up.

The opposite is true, as well. If I have endless endurance, but lack the knowledge of where I'm running to and what my goal is, I will end up wasting my time and my energy. I must continue to mix passion and purpose, knowledge and desire, human grit and heavenly grace. Then I will finish the race triumphantly.

Some people get discouraged when relapses of past mistakes and tendencies take place. The enemy makes them think that they have to go all the way back to the starting point of their journey. So, feeling helpless, they decide to quit altogether. In reality, their relapse only pushed them back a few feet. All they needed was a moment of encouragement to continue.

When I was a kid, I remember watching television shows that would end with a cliffhanger. To pique your interest for the next week, the shows' producers would write "to be continued" on the screen. And so it is with the Christian life. We come to cliffhanging moments of fear, frustration, or failure. It seems that the end will be terrible. But then our faith ascends. We know the journey will not end in defeat, even though it may look that way right now. But we have confidence that the purpose of God will be fulfilled in our lives.

Jesus told his disciples in Matthew 17:20, "If you have faith as a grain of mustard seed, you can say unto this mountain Remove and be cast into the sea, and it shall remove, and nothing shall be impossible unto you."

It starts with a grain. That grain is planted. What is planted grows toward greatness. Faith is exemplified in this principle of perseverance. It may appear at first to be insignificant, but once you have planted your faith in a certain area, watch it grow; observe the development of your miracle. Every day you go into the field of expectations, don't be discouraged by the slowness of your progress. Be motivated by the knowledge that you're getting closer to the fulfillment of your dream.

When faith begins to operate, it speaks to the obstacle. But you can't just speak. You have to watch it be removed. Some people get discouraged because when they spoke a Word of faith, nothing happened. So they walk away. Rather than the mountain finding a new location, the people left. So, the wrong thing moved. You have to continue standing firm after the Word is spoken, and wait for that mountain to be removed.

But it doesn't stop there. Jesus didn't finish His teaching with the removal of the mountain. He went on to say that "nothing shall be impossible unto you." Jesus was explaining that once the obstacle is removed, a new dimension of faith exists. Could it be that the real mountain is not external, but internal? Maybe this mountain is one of insecurity; once it is removed, you are freed to do the ministry God intended for you.

Changing our perceptions is another key to continuing. The devil may have a dead end sign posted on your road, fooling you into thinking it would be a waste of time to continue. But if you look closer, you'll discover that it's not a dead end at all, but a small roadblock. The road does not end with a drop-off into the ravines of spiritual peril. The road continues. It just twists and turns for a few more miles. So now you decide to remove the roadblock. You remove the mentality that you can't go any farther in a relationship, on a job, in a church.

The enemy wants to get you stuck in the rut of yesterday. If you were to come upon the Rocky Mountains 200 years ago, you would not find the asphalt path leading through the dangerous granite shoulders that is there today. You would see wilderness. You would find an impasse. You would have to either turn around or chance treacherous terrain on foot. But that was 200 years ago. We are not living in that day. Nowadays, an adequate route exists to get people through the mountains — white dashes, yellow lines, and steep-grade signs—all of these things tell you that someone else has been here before. Many have made the same journey hundreds of times.

Don't let the past define your boundaries. Don't take a horse-and-buggy mentality on the road to promise when God has designed your faith to speed along in an SUV. A few years ago, you may have been ill-equipped to handle certain tasks in the Spirit. But after trials and tests, with faithfulness and determination, you have grown to a place where access is now possible.

Maybe, in the past, you couldn't talk about an incident of childhood abuse. The memory was too excruciating, and replaying the emotions too difficult. But as time passed, you found freedom from those painful memories. Now, you no longer dwell on the past, living within the confines of your pain, but you move forward, developing as a disciple. The road to emotional stability has been paved smooth.

Maybe you said something insensitive in a leadership meeting some time ago. The fallout was disastrous. You withdrew into a condemnation-infested cave. You didn't think you would ever be able to work with people again. You were afraid the same mistakes would arise, the same hurtful words would slip off your tongue again.

But after a bit of honest self-analysis, and as time heals your emotions, you can leave the historical landmarks of failure where you once settled and explore the avenues of mature ministry. And as you move ahead, you realize that not only have you learned a lot from the experience, but your newfound wisdom would be worthless to anyone else if you had stayed stranded in a negative view of yourself. Now, you are the leader you always dreamed you could be.

I remember being hurt a few years ago by another preacher. I didn't think I would ever be able to discuss the matter without experiencing those bitter emotions again. Any time his name was mentioned, I had to battle bitterness. But eventually I realized the power of forgiveness. And having made a conscious decision to move on, I was able to pull up stakes of hindrance, pack away old unhealthy thoughts, and continue my journey. The dead end was really a roadblock for me. And when I cleared away the corrosive materials of vindictiveness, I saw there was a bridge of healing built beyond the grievance.

I can now talk about this incident without digging at an old scab and reopening a wound. Healing has come. I have stepped beyond the limitations of my past and into the continuing development of my character.

The "and" of Your Faith

I Peter 1:9 states, "Receiving the end of your faith, even the salvation of your souls" (KJV). This verse speaks more of the future reward for faith that endures, for the one who continues to the end. So I think the "and" of your faith is implied here.

What do I mean by this? Often times, you might put a period at the end of your struggle's sentence. Maybe you feel like quitting. You are tired of wrestling with the same issues, the same inadequacies. Or maybe you put an exclamation point there, emphasizing the anger that you feel with each new disappointment.

I say, erase the final punctuation mark and create a plan to continue your journey. Put an "and" into your circumstance.

In Exodus 3 we find a perfect example of this:

And Moses said unto God, Who am I, that I should go unto Pharaoh, and that I should bring forth the children of Israel out of Egypt? And he said, Certainly I will be with thee; and this shall be a token unto thee, that I have sent thee: When thou hast brought forth the people out of Egypt, ye shall serve God upon this mountain" (vs.11-12 emphasis mine).

The "and" brigade begins with Moses questioning his ability to lead Israel, but you have to keep reading. God affirms Moses' calling by telling him where to lead Israel after they come out of Egypt. But it doesn't end here.

And Moses said unto God, Behold, when I come unto the children of Israel, and shall say unto them, The

151

> *God of your fathers hath sent me unto you; and they shall say to me, What is his name? what shall I say unto them? And God said unto Moses, I AM THAT I AM: and he said, Thus shalt thou say unto the children of Israel, I AM hath sent me unto you* (vs.13-14).

So we continue the story with God encouraging Moses, giving him the revelation of His name. This could have been a good place for Moses to stop — right at the door of divine exposure. The One who has always existed has just made Himself known to Moses in a way no one else on earth has ever seen Him.

At that point, Moses might have said, "That's it. I don't want to go any further. I have heard all I need to hear. I can just retire here at Mt. Horeb in the shadow of this great revelation." But God was not finished with the "ands" of Moses' calling:

> *And God said moreover unto Moses, Thus shalt thou say unto the children of Israel, The LORD God of your fathers, the God of Abraham, the God of Isaac, and the God of Jacob, hath sent me unto you: this is my name for ever, and this is my memorial unto all generations. Go, and gather the elders of Israel together, and say unto them, The LORD God of your fathers, the God of Abraham, of Isaac, and of Jacob, appeared unto me, saying, I have surely visited you, and seen that which is done to you in Egypt:*

> *And I have said, I will bring you up out of the affliction of Egypt unto the land of the Canaanites, and the Hittites, and the Amorites, and the Perizzites, and the Hivites, and the Jebusites, unto a land flowing with milk and honey.*

And they shall hearken to thy voice: and thou shalt come, thou and the elders of Israel, unto the king of Egypt, and ye shall say unto him, The LORD God of the Hebrews hath met with us: and now let us go, we beseech thee, three days' journey into the wilderness, that we may sacrifice to the LORD our God (vs.15-18).

So, now we are several more "ands" into the story. Great progress has been made. The elders of Israel are going to come together. The vision of the end of affliction is clearer, the bonds of slavery soon to be the rusty chains of the past. Moses could have interjected, "God, can we please stop here? I like the way this is now." Yet again, God had more "ands" for Moses' consideration:

And I am sure that the king of Egypt will not let you go, no, not by a mighty hand (v. 19).

Uh-oh! This "and" leads to rejection. What happened to the rosy-colored descriptions of all the good things that were going to happen? Why did God have to throw in a contentious Pharaoh? The trail of purpose is not without the tears of predicament. But you can't get stranded at the barricades of resistance. You have to believe beyond the blockage. You have to concentrate on the fulfillment of God's intentions. The enemy of your faith will make you think that the roadblocks, the seemingly insurmountable odds will keep you from going any farther. But look out! Here come a few final words:

And I will stretch out my hand, and smite Egypt with all my wonders which I will do in the midst thereof: and after that he will let you go.

And I will give this people favour in the sight of the Egyptians: and it shall come to pass, that, when ye go, ye shall not go empty (vs. 20-21).

The "and" journey, the journey of continuation, of not giving up, leads us to the place of fulfillment. "Ye shall not go empty." God finishes this outline of future events by showing Moses that the "end of the ands" arrives at a place where Israel leaves Egypt, not only with great deliverance from the taskmasters and wounds of persecution, but also with great treasure.

Throughout this book you have witnessed many stories of triumph through trouble. As you continue on your journey of faith, remember that your destiny is greater than your dilemma. Your impossibility zone doesn't have to be a place of paralyzing fear; rather it is a place for God to show you the wonders of His power and love.

The impossibility zone is truly the place where faith triumphs. Why? Because God reveals Himself through faith. And when God gets involved in the impossibility zone, it soon becomes a great testimony of amazing feats, awesome victories, and undeniable grace.

I once heard an old proverb that I want to leave with you. "Roads are not made for destinations but for journeys." Let's go forward and enjoy the journey!

TO CONTACT THE AUTHOR
website: DannieHoodMinistries.com
e-mail: Danniehood@comcast.net
or call: 303-683-3525